The Little Book

Sia Mohajer

Contents

Hello Mr. Wheeler

On a beautiful Pittsburgh morning in 1995, McArthur Wheeler decided to rob a bank. Not just one bank but two. He chose two large banks located downtown: Fidelity Savings Bank and a Mellon Bank. McArthur had a secret plan; one that he thought would make him exceptionally successful. It involved something very sour—a lemon.

McArthur had just recently discovered "invisible ink". Lemon juice, a substance commonly used in elementary science class, is invisible when used as ink on paper. It only becomes visible when it's heated. Unfortunately for McArthur, his ingenious plan involved covering his face in lemon juice and then robbing the banks. The fact that his face was not made of paper didn't discourage McArthur in his belief that some lemon juice on his face would make him invisible to all the surveillance cameras. Unsurprisingly, several hours after the two robberies, McArthur was in custody. To his astonishment, his plan was unsuccessful. He even protested to detectives, "But I wore the juice."

McArthur had apparently tested his theory before proceeding with his ingenious robberies. In an interview with Sergeant Wally Long, he explained that he had covered his face with lemon juice and used a Polaroid camera to take a picture of himself before the robbery. The picture didn't come out, which was taken as a solid confirmation of this theory. Sergeant Wally Long later speculated that McArthur used bad film or that he had put so much lemon juice into his eyes he wasn't able to use the camera correctly.

Mr. Wheeler's story almost seems fake. How could any human think that he alone had discovered a magic recipe for being invisible; a secret that had been lying under the noses of all humanity in the form of elementary science experiments.

I bring up the story of the amazing Mr. Wheeler to make three points. The first is that all areas of life, success and satisfaction depend on knowledge, wisdom and knowing which rules to follow. This is not only true for violations of the law but also for tasks in social and intellectual domains. This includes areas such as raising children, working, leadership, study and constructing rational arguments. The second is that people differ widely in their knowledge and the strategies they apply in different domains. Each strategy contributes to a varying level of success—with Mr. Wheeler being a particularly poignant example. Some of the knowledge and theories people apply to their actions are sound and produce favorable results. Others, like the lemon juice hypothesis of McArthur Wheeler, are totally wrong, incompetent and sometimes just plain stupid.

Engaging in actions, which we might consider stupid later on is normal. Our personalities and values are not static entities and a future self may look down upon actions of the past. However, what about the people who fail to see that what they are doing is stupid? This brings me to my third point.

When people are incompetent in the strategies they adopt to achieve success, they suffer a dual burden. They not only make mistakes that others may deem stupid but their incompetence robs them of the ability to comprehend it. Instead, they are left with the erroneous impression, like

Mr. Wheeler, that their actions are acceptable and potentially ok.

David Dunning and Justin Kruger

The inspirational story of Mr. Wheeler came to the attention of two Cornell University professors: David Dunning and Justin Kruger. They found the story so compelling that they decided to engage in a series of related experiments. Dunning and Kruger believed that ignorance of standards of performance lie behind a great deal of incorrect self-assessments of competence. Their experiments ranged from operating vehicles to playing tennis. Their research showed that for any given skill, incompetent people generally fail at four key points. They fail to recognize their own ability or skill level. They fail to understand and recognize the skill in others. They fail to understand the level of their incompetence. Finally, they fail to recognize their own lack of the skill, even after they are exposed to training for that skill.

They called it the Dunning Kruger Bias and it's been widely studied. It has been found to affect people in all walks of life with some frightening implications. From law to medicine, history is replete with examples of the Dunning Kruger Bias. However, it is not the only example of "stupidity" quantified by science. There are others.

Enter The Godfather of Biases: Daniel Kahneman

Since the early 1970s, Nobel Prize winning American psychologist Daniel Kahneman has been working hard to understand why we make the mistakes we do. Along with several colleagues, most notably Amos Tversky, he has conducted a multitude of experiments that chronicle all the ways in which we can be stupid.

A bias, put simply, is a systematic pattern of deviation from the norm in judgment. This deviation causes people to make inferences about other people and situations in a highly illogical fashion. People create their own "reality" from selective input. They don't see the whole picture but rather only selected portions of it. It is not the reality of the situation that dictates an individual's behavior but rather his constructed "subjective-social reality". This is the cause of all manner of cognitive biases.

The most interesting part of Kahneman's findings were not how pervasive biases were but rather how adaptive they were. In many contexts, cognitive biases may lead to more effective actions. In situations where time is more important than accuracy, biases serve as powerful "rules of thumb". These "rules of thumb" were later called heuristics, or mental shortcuts. The resulting conclusion is powerful; cognitive biases are a natural result of human processing limitations resulting in limited information processing or, in many cases, lack of appropriate logic.

Basically the research has shown that bias play a fundamental role in allowing us to navigate the world more easily. They provide a sense of meaningful blindness in order to create a reality that can be more easily understood. The example of Mr. Wheeler stands as an extreme example of an otherwise daily "human" system.

Our Constructed Reality: The Movie of You

We are never sure what we really want, and at times, our whole existence seems like an elaborate self-constructed play. Our lives are a constantly intertwining and morphing narrative that ebbs and flows like a river adjusting itself to every context. Each of us is a storyteller whether we know it or not. Our subjective reality is constructed within our minds regardless of what is happening outside.

This book is about the rift between reality and perception. In many ways, they exist as two separate entities only rarely skimming across the surface of each other. Why are they so distant? The reason is simple. You are a story. Your life is a story. Everything you do fits into that story. Within that story, we have a character.

This isn't some random idea I just came up with; rather, it's a well-supported theory of psychology. It's called self-perception theory. It goes a little something like this, "people determine their attitudes and preferences by interpreting the meaning of their own behavior." Our behaviour has to fit somewhere, and that somewhere is our ever-changing, ever-so-adaptable narrative story about who we are.

Every character has a self-image that is raised high in the air for the world to see. Our self-image is supported by our behaviour, opinion and perspective. It's sort of a feedback loop. You do something nice for someone, focus on how nice of a thing you did, and think to yourself, "You did something good today!" Now think of this process going backwards. You decide your attitude by interpreting the meaning of your own behavior. Look! I did something nice today. It must mean I'm truly a nice person. This flexibility in the interpretation process is where cognitive biases are incubated. Interpreting information is a tricky subjective business.

Our behavioral interpretations create a standard of self-conduct that is reinforced by common culture and societal values. If our behaviour does not match our self-image, we create cognitive dissonance (feeling bad). If you see yourself as a law abiding citizen, breaking the law doesn't conform with your self-image. This is a recipe for a moral conundrum. The natural reaction for this heavy burden is to strengthen our support structures.

"In critical moments, men sometimes see exactly what they wish to see." Spock

This is not my quote, but rather Mr. Spock's. Spock would have the clarity to preserve his opinion from the contamination of human emotionality and irrationality. To do this is SO difficult that we even have a regimented, highly controlled method for doing so. It's called the scientific method and it takes a long time to learn and use. Even when we do use it, there needs to be a team of people watching out for subtle biases, and even then, most of the time research is still biased.

Our brains are remarkable, wondrous things that have evolved for one simple reason—survival. Regardless of whatever method ancient man used to survive, our brains have morphed into supercomputers that can take the unending sea of information in the world and make it simple. To be conscious of even a small percentage of all the information that our brains take in would be blinding.

Instead, our automatic processes take in everything and only stream the information that fits within our model of the world. This is referred to as mental accounting. A good accountant doesn't bore you with every detail of the process, but rather gives you the end numbers which you care about. Our brains work the same way.

Brain Corp

Can you image if you were the boss and you had fifteen employees constantly giving you endless information, emails, TPS reports and other miscellaneous crap? You would be overwhelmed with the amount of information that you were receiving. Something would have to be done. You would have to create a policy or a system to limit the information coming in. Anything that didn't fit within that system would be ignored. As a boss you would create a culture for your company.

We are a company, Brain Corp, and we are a responsible, fair, people-centered company. The employees, recognizing this culture and standard, would begin to filter only information that fit this narrative. Again we see our behaviour trying to live up to the expectations of our self-image, like an obedient boy trying to impress his stern father.

Sometimes, the employees at Brain Corp are faced with a complex difficult decision. Since their information is biased towards their narrative, employees often avoid complex decision-making and make an easier judgment based on biased information.

In case I've lost you with all my psychology jargon, I'm talking about your brain. Actually, all our brains. Basically, what I'm trying to say is that our brains are tricking us. Not maliciously but rather automatically, like a grandmother who pours another helping of her high-calorie home cooking on your plate the second you look away. You know she doesn't mean to hurt your body by overeating but rather wants to help you. In an attempt to simplify the world and make it conform to our expectations, we have been blessed with the gift of cognitive biases. Our subjective biases ensure that for as long as humans exist together, we will experience a lifetime of idiots, morons and stubborn people—each experiencing the same event and interpreting it entirely differently.

Be Warned! Seeing How Biased You Are Is Dangerous

Sorry. One more analogy. You are a house. I'm a house too. My name is Sia Mohajer. I'm a 31-year-old elementary school teacher. I believe in blank, blank and blank. This is my identity and I need to protect it. I have made certain ideological commitments and created belief systems which serve to function as my understanding of how society works and should work. Outcomes are understood as a function of my knowledge. This is the foundation of my house. It is the support structure that goes deep into the ground and holds the whole thing together.

My culture is how I navigate the house. If I were a computer, my culture would be my operating system. Our houses need to be strong and survive any big bad wolves who attempt to blow them down. No one would willingly take down their own house. No one would jeopardize the entire structure by curiously digging around its supporting columns in an attempt to understand how they work. We are programmed to protect our houses.

The problem is when we start to really become aware of our own biases. We see that our house isn't as sturdy as we previously believed. Some parts of it may be uneven, poorly constructed or even thrown together. If we look too hard, we might break one of our houses' windows exposing us to the cold reality outside.

Don't get me wrong. I'm not saying we are purposely deceiving ourselves and living in an entirely fictitious reality. I just wanted to make an analogy to show that sometimes seeing errors in your own thinking is detrimental to your own self-impression. We have built our self-impression up and most of us see ourselves as competent and fair. As a result, we expect this same level of competence and fairness from others. We scoff at people who display inferior cognitive skills and feel absolutely indignant when faced with unfairness. Inequality triggers a visceral reaction for most people.

Mommy, Look What I Can Do

Building confidence in kids is one of the most important jobs for a parent. We have all seen children whose parents haven't instilled one iota of confidence in their children. As a teacher, I can tell you, those children are some of the most difficult to work with. Even when they are faced with a problem that they've previously completed well, they will still believe they are unable to complete it again.

Good parents instill confidence in children. This, "believe and achieve" motto serves to kindle their ambition and is somewhat of a recursive process. In fact, what parents are instilling in their children at a young age is an *illusory confidence*. They'll praise a child for tying their shoes even if they did it totally wrong. The same with lunch. Parents will give praise to a child for making their own lunch even if it's just mayonnaise and white bread.

Instilled illusionary confidence is like a set of training wheels. If you don't have them, you'll take a couple of huge spills and that's the end of your biking career. The problem is that illusionary confidence is embedded so deeply, it extends its stupid little fingers all the way into adulthood. I'm sure we have all met confident idiots who believe they can do anything despite a plethora of information indicating they clearly can't. In other words, biases are built into our system from such an early age that finding them can be tricky and even a little dangerous.

How Can You Be SO Stupid?

Have you ever had an argument with someone where the driving force behind the argument is an uncontrollably powerful, "How can they be so blind?" Other people's biases are always ripe for judgment, but rarely do we afford ourselves the same pleasure.

It's in these times of utter frustration that we are given a truly powerful moment to transcend our otherwise overly irrational human selves. You might, just for a second, see how our own decision-making processes are a product of incomplete and limited information. Once you have seen this a few times, the illusion of your knowledge or competence will be challenged.

Let's Get Started

In the next seventy-five or so pages, I'm going to present you with ten of the most common cognitive biases. Whether you know it or not, these biases affect you every day. I'll start every bias off with two situations where you can see the bias in action. As you read the various situations, try to think of a time when you might have experienced a similar problem. After that, we'll talk about the bias itself. Biases are a well-researched field in both social and cognitive psychology.

There is a lot of great information and research which I will share with you. I'll show you exactly how each one of these biases can affect your decision-making processes and how they could be directly affecting your personal life and business decisions. Finally, we will conclude with a little ten-point exercise. The exercise will include ten different scenarios where you must guess which cognitive bias the person is suffering from and how they could think more clearly.

I hope by the end of this book you'll have a greater appreciation for the important role that cognitive biases play in our decision-making processes. Being aware is just the first step to thinking more clearly and becoming more compassionate towards your fellow human beings. If you understand biases within your own life and see how automatically they arise, it will give you a greater understanding of others.

I hope that by reading this short book you will begin to bridge the gap that exists between reality and your perception of it.

One last thing. Now you might be wondering why is this book so short—only seventy pages to explain the intricacies and subtle nature of cognitive biases. You may be thinking that the author must be either a genius or a distinguished scientist. I can assure you of my very average level of intelligence and modest science background. No. This book is short because it's an appetizer. A little apéritif to see if you like the taste. Some of you might not like it. If you want some longer books from great authors about the same subject, I will include them at the end of the book.

So as we start this mini-journey into clearer thinking and understanding why we are all a little stupid, here is one more quote from that great philosopher, Mr. Spock.

"Logic is the beginning of wisdom, not the end." Spock: Leonard Nimoy (1931–2015)

Anchoring

Scenario 1: It's Sunday and Judy is doing her favorite thing—shopping. She's looking for a pair of new shoes, but she isn't sure of the exact style she wants. The prices all seem to strike her as fairly expensive until she finally finds a beautiful pair of blue high heels. The price has been marked down from $129.99 to $69.99. She thinks it's a great deal with more than $60 off the original asking price. She buys them immediately and proceeds to tell her friends about the great deal she got.

Scenario 2: Steve has been thinking about getting a personal trainer for the last several weeks. He initially thought that a monthly price range of $125–$150 was reasonable, but he hadn't inquired about the actual prices yet. Upon asking the gym about the pricing plans, he was shocked by the cost for a month of personal training—$300 a month. After expressing his shock, the sales staff then introduced a more affordable plan at $179.99 a month. After some consideration, he purchased the second plan at $179.99 a month despite the fact that it was more expensive then what he previously wanted.

"Cocaine is God's way of saying you're making too much money." Robin Williams

How quickly we can go from feeling invigorated by getting a "good deal" to feeling somewhat ripped off when we do a quick check online and see that the price we just paid was actually not a discounted price. Rather, it was the standard price, or even worse, more expensive. It almost makes you not even want to look at prices for your recent purchase for fear of seeing the same thing even cheaper.

I had this feeling a few weeks ago while buying a watch. I purchased the watch and then, for some regrettable reason, looked it up on Amazon only to find that it was $50 cheaper than what I had paid for it. This weird flaw in our logic is called anchoring.

Anchoring is one of the fundamental tenants of salesmanship. Making an initial offer at an overly inflated price will influence customers into thinking other lower priced goods are priced more affordably. In other words, the anchoring bias makes us rely too heavily on the first piece of information which will subsequently affect all other decisions. This not only affects monetary transactions but any situation where the first piece of randomly encountered information influences any future decisions. This is especially effective if we enter into a situation with no previous knowledge of the average cost.

If you've ever bargained at a traditional Asian or African market, you'll know that sellers always go ridiculously high with their initial offer. They usually do this to make you accept a price that is higher than average. If you aren't accustomed to this, you're in for an expensive shopping trip.

I remember once asking a carpet vendor sitting next to me in a popular kabob restaurant in downtown Istanbul which tourists were the easiest to sell to. Without blinking or stopping to swallow his kabob, he replied, "Americans." The reason is clearly cultural with initial prices being so high most North Americans just tend to accept the second "best" price.

"There are worse things in life than death. Have you ever spent an evening with an insurance salesman?" Woody Allen

Perhaps this method is a little more blatant and transparent but the same logic applies to salesmanship anywhere. The discounted price you see on the label, or the knocked-down price you see in Walmart, are all examples of the anchoring bias. The perceived value of the discounted item may appear greater than it was previously. If this effect is combined with a limited time offer, it's even more powerful.

It's a basic marketing 101 technique that really works regardless of the customer. The same principle is even used in hostage negotiations. Think of the hostage taker requesting an airplane for the getaway. In the end, he might only get an old minivan with police hidden inside.

You might be thinking, not me. I'm a veteran shopper who can sniff out a bad deal a mile away. Not so fast. Knowledgeable people are not immune from the anchoring bias. In a study by Northcraft and Neale[1] comparing decision-making skills of students and experienced real estate professionals, researchers gave both groups access to listing prices of various homes. Participants were then asked to make offers and then talk about why they made that offer.

Results indicated that despite denying the anchoring effect, both groups were influenced by the initial listing prices. Even when told about this effect, it may be difficult to avoid. Larger purchases are also subject to this bias.

Researchers Janiszewski and Uy[3] conducted an experiment in which they attempted to determine the precision effects of using an anchor. People were asked to make an offer on a beach property using a specific and nonspecific anchored amount ($800,000 vs. $765,450). People who were given the specific anchor (800K) adjusted their estimates of the house value much more than those who were given a nonspecific one. Researchers concluded that anchoring not only affects a starting value but also the starting scale—your initial starting point. A specific price will not result in as much variation and people will adjust to a final price similar to the initial one.

Another more recent example of this effect occurred in 2010 when Apple's Steve Jobs unveiled the newest iPad at $999 but quickly changed the price to $499. People thought, "Wow, that's half the initial price. I better go buy one." Combine this with a limited time offer and you have a recipe for lots and lots of sales.

"We don't know where our first impressions come from or precisely what they mean, so we don't always appreciate their fragility." Malcolm Gladwell

Anchoring is also the bias that helps us form first impressions of people. These impressions aren't easily changed. Our first encounter with a person generally determines how we view that person from then on. Our impression of him or her is anchored by the initial feeling or experience.

Even when we are aware of the power of this bias, it may be extremely difficult to avoid. Focusing on one aspect of any situation may entirely distort our perception. This bias is known as focalism and works in the same way as anchoring.

Focalism occurs when we get so caught up in trying to predict some future event that will determine our happiness that we fail to see our current reality. You can see this affect all the time and I'm sure after a few minutes of reflection, you can think of a decision which you initially thought would make you quite happy but, in fact, didn't. We are terrible predictors of our future states of happiness or welfare.

Living in Canada for most of my life, I have thought countless times about how much happier and healthier I would be if only I could move to sunny California. However, such ambitions are slightly myopic as they don't consider the myriad of other potential happiness influencers. Instead, I get so focused on the most positive aspect, the sun, that I forget to consider everything else as thoroughly.

One study asked people this same question. Participants were asked to choose which group was happier: Californians or Midwesterners. Both groups chose Californians as the happier group because of the pleasant weather. Actual results showed that there was no difference between the actual self-assessed happiness rating of both groups. The bias was caused because people focused on the sunny weather to the exclusion of all other factors[2].

Anchoring our decision or evaluation of an outcome on one overly positive focal point can be misleading. A pay raise at work seems extremely appealing; however, the associated responsibility, work time and stress may detract from its initial perceived value. Sometimes, just thinking about how fun or great something will be is better than experiencing the actual reality of it.

However, the opposite may also be true as well. Focusing on how unpleasant an experience may be could frighten and intimidate people from trying it. How many times have you focused on how painful something will be only to find out that it wasn't that bad after all? You then rejoice in the feeling of taking on the challenge of completing the seemingly difficult task.

Anchoring and focalism are built into our system of thinking. When information is limited or the process of gathering information is difficult, this cognitive bias serves as a time-saving mechanism to help us make decisions fast and effectively. When there is a plethora of information, we tend to latch onto the first piece of info for safety. The problem is a lot of times those decisions just aren't good ones. We rely too much on initial information and become influenced by it.

If you are thinking you are just simply too smart to be fooled like this, think again. Researchers[4] have shown that even those with high cognitive abilities are still willing to pay for expensive anchored consumer goods. However, a method to help you is at hand. Literally, it's in your hand.

Smart phones offer the ability to connect to a huge world of information that allows us to stop and reconsider the initial price using price comparison websites, review websites or reading customer comments. Consulting with another person may be a great idea but only if they weren't subject to the same initial anchoring effect.

Now that you are aware of this bias, I'm sure you will begin to see it everywhere. From price negotiations to Walmart prices to first impressions, ask yourself if your decision is a logically sound one or perhaps one that is slightly too optimistically impulsive. And remember, focalism or anchoring can also work in reverse. It can discourage us from doing tasks which may be extremely beneficial but have a perceived initial painful point of entry.

I'd like to issue a challenge. In the next week or so, see how many times you can see anchoring taking place. The next time you are in any sort of retail setting, be aware of it. You'll be surprised at how common it is.

Confirmation Bias

Scenario 1: As part of her thesis work, Judy has been asked to write a dissertation extolling the virtues of a certain teaching style. She spends three months collecting information and doing research about her subject. Her research topic is integrated classrooms where learners of all abilities work together. The problem is that she has totally failed to consider information that goes against her position. Her research has only found information that confirms her beliefs.

Scenario 2: Steve is a reporter and has been covering a story about a new local candidate. Steve's news station already supports this candidate and all the people who are interviewed either currently work or have worked with this individual. The story is biased from the start. Any information that finds its way into the final report will be subject to serious confirmation bias.

"Facts are stubborn, but statistics are more pliable."
Mark Twain

This is the bias that makes arguing with people really, really, really annoying. Why? Because most people think they know what they are talking about. The problem is you also think you know what you are talking about. So what usually happens when you encounter this dilemma? Naturally, the next logical step is to assume that they are either mentally deficient, damaged or purposely being stubborn. How can they not see the clear impeccable logic in your argument and see that you're clearly correct. This is a slippery slope and the chances are that both of you are suffering from confirmation bias.

We look for confirmation of our belief, philosophy or opinion in all contexts and situations. We find scenarios which support our bias and then stick to those scenarios, regardless of how terrible our argument may be. Calling someone "closed minded" would be a manifestation of the confirmation bias.

The confirmation bias is so fundamental to your development and your reality that you might not even realize it is happening. We look for evidence that supports our beliefs and opinions about the world but excludes those that run contrary to our own.

Confirmation bias is the support structure that holds our beliefs in place. Pondering how reasonable your assumptions are is a tricky business. There is a natural tendency to not want to disturb this status quo and for good reason.

Our confirmation biases often conform to the biases of others who exist within the same micro and macro context. Let me explain further. Your family, cultural background and sociopolitical stance generally agree with those around you. The values and belief systems that unite you are the same ones that we use confirmation biases to actively support. Having a set view of how things are or should be and looking only for information that confirms this view gives way to a self-fulfilling prophecy. If you view yourself as a generous, community oriented, environmentally friendly person, then you will find information or situations in your own life which further support and encourage this way of thinking.

This biased search for information is confirmation bias. As a result, you will see real evidence and examples of how much of a generous, community oriented, environmentally friendly person you are. You'll think, "Wow! It's really true, I'm great!" Hence, it becomes a self-fulfilling prophecy.

"I'm a meathead. I can't help it, man. You got smart people and you've got dumb people." Keanu Reeves

What happens when you encounter someone with a totally opposing set of beliefs? Well, naturally we think he or she is totally crazy or perhaps just too different to understand. Either way, his belief systems are deemed entirely separate from our own.

We need this separation if we don't want to be challenged. One of behavioral psychology's principle tenants is cognitive dissonance. We feel cognitive dissonance when we feel inferior, guilty, ashamed, embarrassed or any other of the multitude of human emotions that makes us want to drink a six pack of beer or eat an entire cheesecake and call it a night. Naturally, we are wired for an innate drive to reduce this dissonance.

As humans, we have expectations or images of ourselves which stem from our historical, cultural and religious foundations. If your actions run contrary to these expectations and your self-image, we experience cognitive dissonance (feeling terrible). Our innate drive towards pleasurable feelings dictates that this dissonance is a big no no. The natural consequence is to either change our actions or, in most cases, manipulate our thinking in order to realign ourselves with our self-image in order to reduce this dissonance. This effect is even more pronounced in intelligent people.

"Smart people believe weird things because they are skilled at defending beliefs they arrived at for non-smart reasons." American author Michael Shermer

Using confirmation bias to defend false, unfair or just plain incorrect beliefs can be seen everywhere. Researchers[5] have found that people frequently search for information that supports their hypothesis or opinion, and they exclude information that doesn't. If we think something is healthy or useful, we generally first search for information of the benefits or advantages and don't immediately jump into a long list of harsh product reviews.

In another study[6], it was found that questions are purposely constructed in ways that already support the hypothesis. This is often referred to as a *positive test* where the outcome is already predetermined by the question. You might have heard the term *loaded question*. This is exactly what this is. For example, asking someone "Have you stopped beating your wife?" contains an implied conclusion that you were already beating her.

Sometimes even slight changes in wording can create dramatic differences. It can affect how people search and process information. Once an opinion is formed, all subsequent searches may be an attempt to support that initial assumption.

One study[7] demonstrated this phenomenon quite clearly. Subjects were asked to rate a person on a scale that measured introversion and extroversion using an interview method. Subjects were given a list of potential questions to ask the interviewee. Before beginning the interview, the person being interviewed was introduced as being introverted or extroverted.

The people who were introduced as being introverted were asked questions such as "What do you find unpleasant about noisy parties?" However, people who were introduced as being extroverted were asked questions such as "How would you liven up a dull party?" The results naturally supported the initial assumption.

Not only is there an active process that encourages confirmation bias, but it's also ingrained within our memory. Our biased memory serves to provide us with a skewed historical account of past occurrences which fall in line with our current mode of cognition. This is referred to as *selective recall* or *access biased memory*.

Schema theory or mental chunking is a theory in neuropsychology which states that information is stored and more easily matched when it fits into previously constructed mental models of reality. Research[8] has shown that information which doesn't match our views of reality is harder to remember or just simply ignored.

Confirmation bias also functions at a neurological level. Contrary opinions or perspectives can create strong emotions that encourage us to defend our beliefs and opinions. Researchers Westen and Pavel[9] found that when subjects made judgments within a magnetic resonance scanner that were contrary to their beliefs, the emotional centers of their brains were activated.

The subjects in Westen and Pavel's study were asked to make statements about presidential candidates. Participants were asked to read positive statements about candidates they disliked. The heightened emotional activity that the researchers recorded in the subjects was attributed to an active attempt to reduce the cognitive dissonance created by reading information that was contrary to their opinion.

Confirmation bias can still persist even when information discrediting a specific viewpoint is present. This sounds totally bizarre, but people do it all the time. I'm sure we all know people who hold certain views that exist without ANY evidence. Encountering people like that can make your brain physically hurt. You feel obliged to show them how erroneous their judgement is.

Research has shown that attempts to "enlighten" believers can be either entirely useless or serve to bolster their current belief systems. This bolstering of belief is often referred to as *entrenching*. This is the idea that once you have invested mental energy into a habit or belief, you strongly reject any potential contradictory information.

I remember trying to convince my grandfather that the ridiculous amount of vegetable oil he was cooking with could be replaced by a healthier alternative, like coconut oil or natural butter. Despite explaining why making the switch would be beneficial for him. It was met with an, "I've been doing this for twenty years and it's served me just fine" kind of comment. Call it stubbornness or entrenchment, the result is the same—not adapting our behaviour to the reality of the situation.

This result has been replicated in the scientific literature. In one experiment, subjects were shown fake experiments. They were then presented with fictitious evidence for a hypothesis. Subjects were thoroughly convinced by the fake hypothesis. Scientists administered two assessments. The first was when the fake hypothesis was presented, and the second was after participants were clearly shown that the entire experiment was false. Results showed that although they were clearly shown that the entire experiment was false, participants still somehow believed that the first fictitious hypothesis was true.

Confirmation bias can also extend itself to see correlations that don't exist. The most extreme case of this is a phenomenon known as paradoila. Paradoila is a result of our overly activate, pattern-detecting brains.

If I told you that in 2004 a grilled cheese sandwich that resembled the Virgin Mary sold for $28,000, would you believe me? Often, information is entirely unrelated, yet similarities can still be drawn. This can commonly be seen in what is referred to as positive-positive correlations. This occurs when two outcomes exist at the same time, and despite being only coincidentally related, a strong positive correlation (that A causes B) between the two is often claimed.

One salient example of this is that cold or bad weather causes people to become ill[11]. Attention is focused on the cold weather and it becomes easier to recall they both occurred simultaneously. This selective recall of information biases your judgement.

"All you need in this life is ignorance and confidence, and then success is sure." Mark Twain

Think of overconfidence. Overconfidence to the point where you just *feel it's right*. You might want to avoid this. A long history of evidence has shown confirmation bias to skew decision making in almost every aspect of life. Financial overconfidence has been the engine of many investors losing all their money or retirement savings. How about picking a random stock and hoping it does insanely well? Don't want to reconsider? Sounds like confirmation bias.

Being so invested in one viewpoint can make recognizing any alternative, potentially beneficial reality difficult. Within the medical community, confirmation bias both contaminates research and creates a status quo that is resistant to change. Until medical technologies improved dramatically, think of how long we were using antiqued methods.

Anecdotal evidence often takes precedence and isn't treated with the same critical opinion that scientific evidence receives. Within the legal realm, decisions that have been made can bias any subsequent information as they are interpreted within the context of that initial decision (think of anchoring again and the extrovert/introvert experiment).

One case that comes to mind is that of David Camm who was charged with murdering his wife and children. Camm was arrested three days after the murders. Despite the overwhelming amount of evidence indicating he was not responsible, investigators still were convinced of his guilt. As a result, they only searched for his DNA on evidence recovered from the crime scene. The evidence was not re-examined for another five years and eventually led to his acquittal.

Confirmation bias also plays a huge role in the development of conspiracy theories regarding the paranormal. When there isn't much evidence available, any evidence will do.

It is ironic how confirmation bias can be described as both a building block for confidence and also as a flaw in our cognition. As we grow up, our search for answers and information helps give children the structure and foundation that allows them to confidently explore the world.

The overly confident child is often cute and innocent in his naivety. His confidence allows him to unleash his curiosity and carve out an understanding of life that will serve as a vehicle for his endeavours. If a child's values and belief systems are challenged by powerfully confusing emotional stimuli, it may disrupt his or her natural development.

In other words, confirmation bias is a normal tool for development. It is only in our later years that we really need to become aware of how we support our choices and actions with information that only serves our own purposes.

The more I have paid attention to this over the years, the more I have come to realize that I'm quite stupid and, even more, stubborn. Yes, stupid in the sense that I only want to see what I want to see. I have blinded myself in a way and opening myself up to being totally wrong has enabled me to be more compassionate, humbler and smarter.

Your Mission If You Choose To Accept It

Next time someone offers you a point of view that runs contrary to your own, stop for a second and recognize the need to immediately jump to evidence that supports your own perspective. You don't have to do anything, just recognize how that need arises automatically.

Hyperbolic Discounting

Scenario 1: Judy is a teacher and makes a decent amount of money. At the end of the month, she has an extra $400. She had originally planned on contributing $300 every month to her pension plan. Instead, nearly every month, she spends most of the remaining money. When asked, she says, "It's hard to put things off for so long. I live in the now and just want to enjoy my life." She has been doing this for nearly ten years and has only contributed a very modest sum to her pension plan.

Scenario 2: Steve is done work and drives by In and Out Hamburgers. He knows he shouldn't eat the delicious, double-patty hamburger, but he is too tempted and he gives in. Just one more, he promises himself. The problem is that Steve is overweight—severely overweight. His doctor has been warning him about his increasing blood pressure and cholesterol levels. Steven promises to work harder at the gym next week and decides he should just enjoy the burger now.

Welcome to the wonderful world of hyperbolic discounting. Doesn't it sounds like a really fancy term used in chemistry? Actually, the concept is quite simple. Basically, it means that people value money over time. But not just any time, I mean the here and now. Time-based choices (receiving something now as opposed to later) are no different from one another other than the fact that rewards or consequences are delayed and must be anticipated. This creates hyperbolic discounting.

The discounting aspect originates from the idea that the value must be reweighed or revalued because of the delay.

If that is too complicated, think of getting $5 today as opposed to getting $25 in a year. Which would you choose?

"Patience is bitter, but its fruit is sweet." Jean Jacques Rousseau

Most people want what they want immediately, and I can't blame them. If I were Steve, I would probably eat the hamburger too. The problem is that sometimes getting what we want right away isn't the most logical or best choice for us. Other times it can be downright dangerous (health related).

This ingrained desire to want to maximize pleasure NOW is built into our brains. Neuroscientists have demonstrated that "the true objective of the brain is to maximize the rate of reward."[12]

Hyperbolic discounting and the ability to control oneself in the face of temptation work together. Perhaps the most famous experiment involving this bias was conducted in the 1970s in Stanford. Dr. Walter Mischel offered a group of subjects (children) the choice between two sets of rewards.[13] The children could choose a reward that was offered immediately or wait for fifteen minutes and receive two similar rewards. Rewards came in the form of cookies and pretzels. The children were then observed to see if they would resist the temptation of the immediate prize for the two rewards later on.

Follow up studies[13] indicated that students who were able to wait longer tended to have better lives as measured by educational attainment, health, SAT scores and other life measures. The study emphasized the importance of delayed gratification.

Delaying your desire and waiting for some future reward is a really difficult idea to sell to people. This is especially true given how uncertain the future may be. We all know it's a good idea to save money, but why are most of us still in debt or living paycheck to paycheck? The answer is we just aren't wired for delayed gratification. We want the cookie now. Heck, give us a bag of cookies and we'll sit here and eat them all without moving or chewing.

Evolution has made us instant-gratification machines and our consumer culture of "Just Do It" and "Have It Your Way" serves to support our innate greed for more and more. Even our powerful brains aren't on our side. As a matter of fact, our brains light up like Christmas trees whenever we receive a reward.

Researchers[14] have found that the brain even uses hyperbolic discounting as a learning mechanism. Our basal ganglia which is responsible for reward-based learning and feedback is activated when presented with a rewarding stimulus. Waiting a long time for some distant, better reward won't give us that immediate hit of feel-good neural activity that makes a McDonald's meal taste so good until the regret sets in.

"My one regret in life is that I am not someone else."
Woody Allen

I'm sure everyone can remember their mother telling them that they need to do something or else they'll regret it later. The problem is that when you grow up, you find out that they were actual right the whole time. I've made many decisions in the past that I now laugh at. Hyperbolic discounting tends to make decision making quite inconsistent over time. The choices made today are definitely not the ones your future self might make.

You can see examples of hyperbolic discounting everywhere. Financial decisions are among the most susceptible to this cognitive bias. Credit cards seem to have been designed with this cognitive bias in mind—spend now and be indebted later. The inability to save has almost reached epic proportions in the United States with pre-2008 financial crises savings levels at -0.5 percent!

Intellectually, we know what we SHOULD do and probably how to do it. The problem is making yourself do it. It's difficult to imagine how much happier we would be if we were financially stable or healthy due to a diligent regular investment of energy and time towards a future goal. Goals that are far away sometimes seem too hard to imagine. The distant feeling of reward may be difficult to conceive and not as appealing as an immediate two-hour shopping trip.

If you pay now! You'll receive…

The easiest place to see examples of hyperbolic discounting are in advertising. Anytime you encounter words such as buy now, pay later; get a free gift; no money down or see a price with a longer term and lower price, you'll know this is the impulsive world of hyperbolic discounting.

You can avoid this bias by having a plan and sticking to it. If you feel you're easily swayed into buying things you didn't originally plan on buying, write down your budget for whatever item you wish to purchase.

Consulting with another person is another way to avoid this bias. Asking him or her what they think and having them analyze a potential purchase or investment rationally can help provide some clarity.

Dunning Kruger

Scenario 1: Last Tuesday, Judy was eating lunch with her friend. They were having a lovely time discussing life when the topic of the weather came up. Her friend mentioned global warming and Judy protested by claiming that global warming was false and exaggerated. Upon being asked why, she quoted a privately funded YouTube documentary and two articles she read on Facebook. She was quite confident in her opinion and even challenged her friend to go do some more research.

Scenario 2: Steve has been picking stocks for years. He uses Google finance to research individual stocks and relies on CNN money for hot tips from experts. He thinks he is pretty good at picking stocks that will be successful. He has become known among his friends as "the stock guy." He often gives advice to others and, unfortunately, many have listened to him. Despite his history of losses, he still only focuses on the small amount of appreciating stocks he holds. If you asked Steve, he would say he is an experienced stock picker with a keen eye for securities. The truth of the matter is his returns are far below the market average. If he had just bought an index fund (a mutual fund that buys a small portion of all major stocks within a given sector), he would have done remarkably better. Don't tell Steve that though because he is "the stock guy."

"The whole problem with the world is that fools and fanatics are always so certain of themselves, and wiser people so full of doubts." Bertrand Russell

This is the Dunning Kruger cognitive bias. It is named after Cornell University psychologists David Dunning and

Justin Kruger after they published a series of experiments in 1999. The Dunning Kruger bias occurs when unskilled people believe they are skilled, knowledgeable or exceptionally experienced in something when they're not. Ironically, highly skilled people underestimate their relative ability and think that tasks which are easy for them are just as easy for others.

In other words, most people think they are good at something but actually they're just confident fools. These people use that same confidence to mask their ignorance and incompetence. I'm sure you can think of someone like this! On the other hand, people who are talented or extremely knowledgeable are so humble that they believe their superior ability to be average.

"A fool doth think he is wise, but the wise man knows himself to be a fool." Even Shakespeare knows and he was no fool. The event that inspired Dunning and Kruger's 1999 study[15] involved a bank robber who attempted to cover his face with lemon juice and rob a nearby bank. The robber, McArthur Wheeler, believed that the lemon juice would make his face invisible from the surveillance cameras because lemon juice is a form of invisible ink. Unsurprisingly, he was arrested immediately.

Now you may be thinking that this sounds a lot like confirmation bias. We only want to see what serves our purposes. The two are very similar and both lead to an over-inflated sense of self-esteem. People who suffer from this bias are unable to accept that they are wrong or less intelligent than others.

It seems like such a puzzling idea. One would think that once ignorance is exposed, honesty would then take its place. That doesn't seem to be the case. Most people will just dig in and defend their potentially ridiculous point of view. In a recent article by Dunning [16], he stated, *"What's curious is that, in many cases, incompetence does not leave people disoriented, perplexed, or cautious. Instead, the incompetent are often blessed with an inappropriate confidence, buoyed by something that feels to them like knowledge."*

So the majority of people are confident idiots. I'm sure you're now thinking that you're at the top of that curve. Think of a time when you have had that gut feeling where you KNOW you are right. You just know it. How reliable is that feeling?

After reading and reflecting on my own ignorance for many years, I've become fairly incredulous of that "I know I'm right" feeling. It took a long time and I'm quite sure I've had many moments where I appeared arrogant to others, but I now attempt to pause for a moment and examine my actual knowledge. I ask myself, "What do I actually know for sure? What am I basing this on? Is the information I have valid? What am I assuming?"

You may find that, unfortunately, our perceptions of our own abilities and those of others are not founded on any grounds other than assumptions and anecdotal evidence. However, to think rationally like this takes deliberate effort and time. It can seem that our reality and our perception of it almost function independently of each other. You can see how people would naturally choose to live in the fictional world and only face reality when it was convenient. Dunning[17] has described this condition as "the anosognosia of everyday life". Anosognosia is a physical disability caused by brain injury where patients deny or are totally unaware of the existence of a disability.

"I never let schooling interfere with my education." Mark Twain

Regardless of age or education level, the Dunning Kruger bias can be found whenever self-assessment takes place. From reading comprehension, driving skills, or sports ability, people generally rate themselves higher than others. Even when asked how attractive or intelligent we are, subjects almost always give themselves a score slightly higher than average. This effect has been referred to as the Lake Wobegon Effect. Lake Wobegon is a fictional location *where all the women are strong, all the men are good looking, and all the children are above average.*

When people are asked to self-assess their reasoning skills, humor or grammatical skills, we see overconfidence. In one study[18] , students were shown test scores then asked to estimate their own rank. Skilled students estimated their rank accurately whereas unskilled students overestimated theirs.

This bias also extends itself into professional work where it may be downright dangerous or damaging. Examples of this bias can be seen in the medical and financial community. In 2012, the National Financial Capability Study[19] asked 25,000 financial respondents to rate their own financial knowledge. The self-assessments were then rated for accuracy. Roughly eight hundred participants who had filed for bankruptcy in the last two years scored abysmally low. Despite their total lack of financial knowledge, the participants with the lowest scores actually reported their level of knowledge as higher than the other participants.

You can also see financial ignorance in the events that caused the 2007–2008 financial crisis. This same confidence has been seen within the medical field as well. A 2001 study[20] showed newer doctors were unable to recognize their own incompetence and gave themselves above average scores on various metrics of medical and clinical knowledge.

Subsequent research also showed that lab technicians evaluated their own on-the-job expertise as much higher than it actually was. It's a slightly scary thought to think that even the people who we trust with our health and money can be subject to this bias.

When we examine the actions of those around us, it's sometimes just too easy to see where they were totally wrong or just plain stupid. Others' faults and mistakes seem so obvious that we wonder how they could be unaware of them. However, we rarely turn this hypercritical eye inwards and see how we suffer from the same sense of over-inflated confidence and self-worth. People think that somehow they are different. The problem is, they probably aren't.

I always thought I was fairly introspective and accurate in my own self-assessment, but I didn't realize how much I didn't know until I actually started to know stuff. Throughout my life, I had always believed that I was fairly scientifically minded, that I analyzed information rationally and that I had a decent understanding of biology, chemistry and physics. I prided myself on my knowledge and often jumped into conversations or started arguments based on my facts.

Luckily, I was at least open-minded enough to read, and I read a lot. The one thing that I constantly took away from every book was how much I didn't know. It was a humbling process to face the facts—I was basically an over-inflated bag of nonsense. When I pushed out all the hot air, what was left was nothing but a few axioms of truth. The most important one being that I didn't know as much as I previously thought and neither did anyone else and that was just fine.

Knowing how ignorant I actually was brought a sense of clarity that allowed me to finally see reality much more clearly. Not only did I see my own reality better, but I could see my former ignorant self reflected in the actions of others.

Not having to hold onto that bag of hot, over-inflated air was also a great relief. Overconfidence is something that needs to be defended. You can see this in the visceral reactions of some people when their opinions are challenged. When I feel this anger creeping up within myself, I always use it as a cue to ask myself a few simple questions.

- How knowledgeable about this subject am I really?
- What am I basing my opinions on? Is that source reliable?
- What purpose am I serving by attempting to validate my point at any expense?

You don't have to ask yourself the same questions. When you feel that instant fight or flight response to being challenged intellectually, try being mindful and reflect on your own knowledge as you engage with others.

Sunk Cost Fallacy

Scenario 1: Judy has been with her boyfriend, Paul, for over four years now. To say their relationship is rocky would be a gross understatement. Judy has gotten used to weekly battle royales which leave her feeling insulted, unwanted and hurt. Paul is verbally abusive and doesn't treat Judy with the respect she deserves. Last week, upon telling her best friend about her predicament, Judy explained her reasoning for not being able to leave Paul. She said, "We have been together for four years. We live together and share everything. We can't just give up. I need to find a way to make this work."

Scenario 2: Steve has recently opened a new business; a restaurant to be exact. The problem is the area he has chosen isn't a high-traffic area. He has been steadily losing money for two years now and has borrowed a significant amount of money from his friends and family. Despite the evidence indicating that he won't be successful in the future, he still stays persistent and confident that he will succeed. His relatives have urged him to consider another business but Steve says, "I've already invested so much time and money in this that I can't just quit now."

"Two things scare me. The first is getting hurt. But that's not nearly as scary as the second, which is losing." Lance Armstrong

This is the sunk cost fallacy. People use rational past decisions to justify irrational current decisions. Basically, people justify putting more time, effort or money into something because they have done so in the past. This is despite the fact that evidence indicates continuing the decision will outweigh future rewards.

Sound familiar? We can see it everywhere. From business to our love lives, none of us are safe from this pervasive little bias. Sunk cost isn't just a hyper-persistent behavior but is rather persistence in the face of overwhelming evidence pointing to future failure. The sunk cost fallacy is sometimes referred to as the Concorde fallacy. The word Concorde originated from the Concorde airplane project funded by the British and French governments. The project was continued despite the fact it was losing serious money. It should have been terminated much sooner but instead money was continually pumped in.

Money isn't the sole factor that can escalate levels of commitment. Any form of pressure may contribute to an irrational level of commitment. Social or psychological pressure is also a powerful escalator. Think of relationships. Sometimes, you're in one that you just shouldn't be in. I'm sure many of you have experienced this. I know I have. How many times have you seen two people together and thought why in the hell are they together? It's pretty hard to pull the plug on something that you've spent so much time on; especially, if you still hold an irrational hope that things will change.

I've personally had a relationship where I questioned my own motives but still stayed with the person. The same goes with a job that you've done for years; you feel hesitant and are scared to try something new. You've already spent so much time working hard that you just can't leave. These are all examples of a social-based sunk cost fallacy.

"If winning isn't everything, why do they keep score?"
Vince Lombardi

39

We all hate losing. Some hate it more than others. The future is uncertain and your brain wants you to maximize pleasure and reward now (we talked about this earlier in hyperbolic discounting). In his bestselling book, *Thinking Fast and Slow*, Daniel Kahneman[21] explains that the brain has evolved an automatic, unconscious process system for judging how to proceed when a potential loss or failure arises. Our evolution has programmed us to avoid threats (losses) at all costs and maximize opportunities.

When I say opportunities, I mean the opportunity to pass on our genes. This is what evolution as all about. This has led to genetic programming which encourages people to avoid losses more than it encourages people to seek gains.

This loss-aversion ratio has been replicated many times. While loss aversion or risk aversion is another cognitive bias, it's the fundamental driving force behind the sunk cost fallacy. Not giving up on a project, as Judy and Steve should do, is a form of loss aversion. We have already invested so much time, money, and energy into something that stopping is difficult.

Writer Dan Ariely [22]created an experiment illustrating this. Ariely set up a booth in a crowded university campus. Students passing by could purchase two kinds of chocolates, Hershey's Kisses for one cent or Lindt Truffles for fifteen cents. Most people chose the truffles. Ariely[22] then set the booth up again offering kisses for free and truffles for fourteen cents. This time, surprisingly, most people chose the Hershey's kisses. By lowering the price by one cent, the price difference was in fact exactly the same. If the students acted totally rationally and logically, they would have seen that there was no difference and would have continued to buy the truffles. The problem is we don't think that logically. You might be thinking that people are just cheap.

Let's say you were going to see a movie. The ticket costs ten dollars; however, right before you go into the theater you realize you lost the ten dollars. Would you still buy a ticket? Kahneman[21] found that 12 percent of people would not buy another ticket.

Now think of the same situation. You buy a ticket and are about to hand it over to the door guy, but you lost it. Would you buy another ticket? This slightly altered scenario found that 54 percent of people would not buy a new ticket. Each situation involves spending or losing twenty dollars; however, the second one is somehow much worse. It somehow feels like an even bigger loss if you have decided to spend money on a ticket and then lose the ticket. You can see how logically this makes no sense; it's still twenty dollars either way, but when we assigned a purpose for our money, losing out is much more painful.

"One should always play fairly when one has the winning cards." Oscar Wilde

Have you ever thought to yourself, "I definitely shouldn't finish this extra-large cheeseburger I just bought."? I wasn't even that hungry when I bought it." Despite this, what do most of us do? Well, that's simple. Force yourself to finish all one thousand calories of its fried goodness.

My grandmother used to have an excellent trick for getting everyone to finish their already over-sized dinner portions (portions assigned by her)—she would eat them if we didn't. The sight of seeing my overweight eighty-five–year-old grandmother finishing our plates of food was more than enough to encourage a little overeating. It made perfect sense to her because she didn't want to waste the food. The problem was we could have just as easily put it in the refrigerator.

The sunk cost fallacy escalates situations to levels and in directions that you previously hadn't even conceived of. How about paying an extra six hundred million more than something is worth? This is the exorbitant price that Robert Campeau[23]) paid for Bloomingdale's (department store) after engaging in an ego-driven price war.

Auctions are prime examples of the sunk cost fallacy on steroids. So are wars. Military strategists have continued to throw in money, manpower and, unfortunately, human lives long after doing so is even remotely useful. There have been countless examples of this throughout history from Vietnam to Iraq. Staying until the job is finished isn't so much a matter of pride and honor as it is of bad reasoning. Lives already lost and dollars already spent often become the justifying reason for continued involvement.

We see the same conundrum echoed within our personal lives. I have continued, and greatly escalated, many personal arguments because I believed myself to be correct. Once you have sided with a particular line of reasoning, it's quite difficult to just leave it. You are emotionally and socially invested in that reasoning. You need to stick to your guns, right?

Thinking of the sunk cost fallacy makes me think of Clint Eastwood in the movie Gran Torino. He plays a racist, salty, old war vet who begrudgingly befriends his Asian neighbors. It's a great movie. Eastwood does a fantastic job of struggling between his old, racist ways and opening up to his neighbours. His stubbornness acts as a shield protecting his racist self which he's invested a lifetime of energy into.

It's this same stubbornness that we all see in our own lives; a stubbornness that makes us resistant to change and averse to loss. It always seems to crystallize with age. People don't like changing their habits as they get older. Ironically we don't see this same stubbornness in animals and children.

Studies[25] on small children and lower animals (they aren't related) indicate that they don't commit this same fallacy. Instead, they focus only on immediate losses and gains and don't care about the previous amount of time and energy invested. Adults are better at overgeneralizations. We are excellent at applying a certain rule (Never quit, keep going!). By choosing a simple rule, we learn to avoid bad outcomes.

Fundamental Attribute Error

Scenario 1: Judy is driving. She just finished her long work day and she is stuck behind another car. The driver of the car in front of her is driving erratically. A series of questions come into her mind. What is he doing? Why is he driving so slowly? The natural conclusion is he is probably old. No, no why is he slowing down here? There is no place to turn. Why is he driving in both lanes at the same time? He must be an old man who can barely see over the wheel. He is probably too old to be driving. Judy speeds up to see how old he is and to confirm her suspicion. Instead, she sees a young woman talking on her cell phone as she drives.

Scenario 2: Steve recently finished a meeting. He leaves feeling frustrated and fairly upset. His project manager seemed distant and rude today Steve assumed it must be due to his recent performance. Steve blames himself for working badly and also feels that his manager was rude, inconsiderate and unprofessional. He spends the rest of the day being both upset and unproductive. Later, he returns home to vent his frustration to his wife. The problem is that the project manager just received a letter from his wife asking for a divorce, but Steve will never know this.

"I have a saying. Never judge a book by its cover. I say that because I don't even know who Ozzy is. I wake up a new person every day." Ozzy Osbourne

I would bet $5 (I don't have much money) that you were subject to this cognitive bias today, maybe even in the last few hours; especially, if you've been in a social environment. This is by far the most common bias and after you've read to the end of this section, you'll begin to see it occurring EVERY day.

A small observation (regardless of how inaccurate it is) leads to a wide generalization. All further judgments are fixed with that label. For example, John is late; therefore, John is inconsiderate and always late. Assigning fixed states or characteristics due to a singular event is an automatic process that we aren't generally cognizant of.

The world is a complicated place and the amount of sensory and social stimuli that our brains have to process is beyond our comprehension. This is the brain's way of categorizing things very, very fast but also very, very inaccurately. We are only left with the option of creating half-cocked hypotheses—just like Judy and Steve.

You may think this isn't fair; but fairness is not an issue when faced with our intrinsic need to create a world that is both safe and controlled. We want to make things understandable and safe and, consequently, easier to assign blame. Attributing failure to a person's personality or character as opposed to the situation is a wonderful way to accomplish this.

Believing that things work in simple linear cause and effect relationships is a lovely convenient fiction. The truth is that the world is extremely complicated and there is no way we can understand a fraction of the events that contributed to another event occurring.

Our personalities aren't static entities but are rather more situational dispositioned than we would like to believe. Believing the world is simple is an idea proposed by Melvin Lerner[26] in 1997. His *just-world hypothesis* explained the belief that people get what they deserve and deserve what they get. This sounds rational enough, right? Believing that things are tidy and neat satisfies our need to see the world as fair and encourages the illusion that we have control. The world is full of perceived threats. The just world helps us find meaning in difficult circumstances.

If anyone has ever witnessed a serious accident, you will know that after the initial shock, we all have this need to assign a reason for the incident and to assign blame. It's part of our coping mechanism. We can't simply discount it as being totally random so we need to establish a motive or reason. This encourages a tendency to blame victims of domestic abuse, rape or accident victims.

I'm sure we can all think of an example of when we were totally wrong about someone. We feel embarrassed about what we might have said earlier. Sometimes we just don't want to think too much, and easy answers to situations are better than exerting the mental effort. Fritz Heider,[27] a psychologist, wrote, "behaviour tends to engulf the field and that perceivers tend to attribute behavior to whatever grabs their attention."

We are cognitively stingy. If our cognitive energy was like magic points in a video game, we would want to conserve it and not think too hard. Our mental cheapness can also been seen within the English language itself.[26] The human lexicon (vocabulary) has more descriptive terms for behavior than it has for describing situations. This focus on behavior over situations makes behavioral dispositions and traits easier to identify.

However, there is an interesting cultural element to this as well. A person's culture can contribute to how prone they are to the fundamental attribute error (FAE). A westerner with a high focus on individualism will naturally concentrate more on individual factors than situational factors. Conversely, people from collectivistic cultures are less prone to FAE. In 2004, Takahiko Masuda created several experiments[28] to illustrate this difference.

In two experiments involving a fish tank and a series of cartoons, their research indicated that Americans will look at focal objects (individual fish, individual faces) while Japanese will look at contexts (plants, rocks, other people's faces). This major difference shows a fundamental difference in cognition; one which makes culture a determining factor for susceptibility to FAE.

Next Time

So the next time you're thinking that driver in front of you is a total jerk for making you wait an extra three to four seconds, you might want to think again. There may be something else going on. The majority of us wouldn't want to be judged so quickly; however, we aren't scared to throw a label on others. I think the biggest thing you can learn is how often you engage in this bias yourself. Knowing how flawed your own thinking is creates an incredible amount of empathy for others. Just remember that people are struggling with the same flawed mental shortcuts. Shortcuts that don't take into account subtle situational factors before making behavioral judgments.

Survivorship Bias

Scenario 1: Judy has been thinking of buying some mutual funds. She has met a local broker and is planning on purchasing a US-based mutual fund. The fund is advertised as having a 6–7 percent return for the last six years. The broker shows her a chart illustrating how her capital and monthly contributions will compound into a handsome sum. She is convinced and invests a large portion of her money. The problem is the mutual fund is a skewed representation. Mutual funds operate a number of funds privately and only after solid performance do they open them up to the public. This is known as an incubation period. Funds with unattractive performance are terminated. The advertised 6–7 percent return is not accurate and only represents two of the top funds that did exceptionally well.

Scenario 2: Steve has been trying to start a side business. He has gone to the library and borrowed a couple of reputable older business books. They stress the importance of a solid business plan. Steve works tirelessly on his plan, and after implementing it at great personal cost a year later, he finds it's basically useless. His product isn't in demand and his marketing methods are all wrong. The problem is that the world has changed since those books were written and the principles in those old books won't work in his industry.

"History is written by the victors." Winston Churchill

We love winners. Winning is awesome. Winning is hard though and it's a lot of work. What is the next best thing to winning? Listening to stories about winning. Welcome to the survivorship bias. This bias occurs when people focus on the success stories of people or things that survived a difficult event instead of looking at those that didn't do quite so well. The survivors are praised and a number of accurate as well as very inaccurate conclusions are placed upon their success. The result is an overly optimistic belief that those people or things hold a magical key to achieving the same level of success.

The problem with this bias is that we ignore the failures and as a result, we ignore valuable insights. We see this bias in education, finance, medicine, law and in the military.

Thank you, Mr. Wald

I'm sure most of you haven't heard of Abraham Wald. I hadn't either, but he saved a lot of lives using everyone's favorite subject—math. Wald, a statistician, used the idea of survivorship bias to minimize bomber losses to enemy fire. A study conducted at the Center for Naval Analyses [29] recommended that armour be added to areas of bomber planes that received the most damage. After putting in some good ol' detective work, Wald decided that since the bombers survived the missions, the armour must already be sufficient. Instead, he decided to add armour to the previously unarmoured areas.

Using some pretty complicated math, he convinced the top military brass that his theory was right. The result was a huge reduction in bombers being shot down. The irony of this example is that the Navy, with a huge inflated wartime budget and tons of manpower, still couldn't see past this simple logical error. It seems simple once you see it, but we are effectively blind to it.

Judy may end up being thoroughly disappointed over her expected annual 7 percent return. I hope she read the super tiny fine print that clearly indicated that the advertised 7 percent return was the result of a biased incubation period that only beat the market temporarily (statistics show that mutual funds almost always underperform the market).

Survivorship bias creates a tendency for failed companies or financial ventures to be wholly excluded from performance studies. This bias was shown by a 1996 study[30]. Researchers Elton, Gruber and Blake concluded the effect is larger in the small funds sector than in larger funds. Biased financial information leads investors to make poor choices. The same bias is seen within the business education industry. Books detailing success stories dominate the shelves. The problem is that, sometimes, companies or people don't really know why they were so successful.

It may even have been a mistake that allowed them to do so well. I'm not discounting all the hard work and skill that it takes to succeed in any industry; however, there is a certain amount of luck or timing that plays a fundamental role in success. Who knows how well a Walmart or a Subway would do if we tried opening it at another time in history. There are always unexpected circumstances that can have a disproportionately large impact on our world.

Author Taleb Nassim refers to these events as black swans. A black swan is a random event that plays a fundamental role in shaping any given outcome.[30] Basically, randomness adds up to unexpected circumstances that could be great or bad. The future is wonderfully unpredictable. If we approach the future only armed with superstitious beliefs about the "right way" to do things, we severely limit our ability to adapt.

In reality, we should be slightly skeptical of any method that promises to duplicate the success of certain individuals. Our biases serve to make the messy world neat and tidy; a place where we can infer laws and rules about how and why things work the way they do. However, this implied underlying structure isn't always true. Once again, we see how reality and our perception of it can function independently of each other.

"The harder you work the luckier you get." Gary Player

This is one of my favorite quotes. Sometimes though, regardless of how hard you work, you always seem to be unlucky. We all have times where several bad things happen to us and we feel extremely unlucky. Psychologist Richard Wiseman studied this phenomenon involving four hundred subjects from various backgrounds.[31] The subjects were chosen after a newspaper ad was placed in a local paper asking for people who considered themselves to be either lucky or unlucky. Over the course of ten years, he requested participants to keep diaries, interviewed them and conducted various tests. In the most notable test, he asked subjects to count the number of photographs inside the newspaper.

Self-labeled lucky and unlucky people had hugely different completion times. Lucky people took a few seconds whereas the unlucky people took two minutes. He later edited the newspaper and inserted a giant block of text on the second page that read, "Stop Counting. There are 43 photographs inside this newspaper." This was followed by an equally large block of text on the follow page that read, "Stop counting, tell the experimenters you have seen this and win $250." Surprisingly, the people who considered themselves unlucky missed BOTH!

You're probably asking yourself how this is possible. Wiseman concluded that "being lucky" is actually a pattern of behavior. It's basically our attitude towards random occurrences. More importantly, it's that initial reaction when we experience something unexpected. Unlucky people crave the security that only a neat and tidy world can provide and as a result tend to be more anxious and narrowly focused. Lucky people just jump right in; they are open to whatever may happen. They aren't as narrowly focused.

The result is that lucky people just experience more events and in a wider variety than intrinsically more anxious people. Lucky people don't require the same security and were attracted to new experiences. The more things you try, the higher your chances of encountering that one thing that really works. So, good luck or bad luck is the result of humans interacting with chance—some people are just better at it than others.

"People call things vulgar when they are new to them. When they have become old, they become good taste."
Mary Quant

We always seem to look at the past as the hallmark of exceptional quality and craftsmanship. We discount the last fifty years of rapid technological growth and innovation. Somehow old things are just cooler and better. Old mustangs are awesome. The Beatles' music is great.

I agree. All of these things are awesome, and that is exactly the reason they survived. Just like now, there was a lot of garbage being produced every day. Luckily, we don't remember most of it. The problem is that we take the old classics and set them up as a standard for all old things. It doesn't work like that.

Humans have always been producing crap. Naturally, we can't remember or even know about all those past products, music or other things that were just plain terrible. The only things that shine through into our modern age of short attention spans and endless distractions are the epic success stories that we internalize as the quintessential paths of success.

Bias Blind Spot

Scenario 1: Judy has been receiving gifts from a certain student's parent. In the past, Judy has spoken about other teachers who receive gifts from parents and how it affects their behavior towards that particular student. Judy said, "It is unfair. Teachers who receive gifts from parents will give that child special treatment. It will affect their decision-making ability." This lunch room conversation was immediately forgotten when Judy received a package of expensive Godiva chocolates one day. She rationalized to herself that she would take the gift, but since she was an intelligent and responsible teacher, it wouldn't affect her judgment in anyway. Whether it did is a different story, but the point was that Judy thought she would be less biased than the other teachers who also viewed themselves as equally responsible and fair.

Scenario 2: Steve was asked to take a test at work to evaluate his level of competence using some new software. He didn't study for the test and doesn't know the software very well. Despite this fact, he is still confident in his ability. He walks into the test room and promptly writes the test. After receiving the results, Steve is shocked. He thinks that perhaps the test was unfair or that they marked it incorrectly.

"We are all born ignorant, but work hard to remain stupid." Benjamin Franklin

I definitely don't have this bias. If there is any bias that I don't have, it's this one. There is no way, I'm writing a book about this stuff, right? Naturally, you're now thinking how exceptionally bias-free you are as well. Clearly, other people lack the superb level of clear thinking we enjoy. They're biased and you can see how irrational others are in their decision making—those idiots.

The problem is that we are all idiots; especially, when we think we are more rational and less prone to biases than others. This is the bias blind spot. It's named after the visual blind spot in our eye (or car). We recognize the cognitive bias of others but fail to see the importance of our own biases on our judgment.

Bias blind spot is a major contributor to other biases. We talked earlier of the human need to create a hyper-inflated sense of confidence and self-worth. We need this to navigate the murky, unpredictable waters of life and to give us some measure of importance in a world where we can sometimes feel so unimportant. We don't like to be reminded of our relative unimportance, our lack of ability or our lack of knowledge. What better remedy for this than to believe that somehow we are luckier, smarter, more able and better looking than all other humans. They are great, but you are just a little bit better; at least, you believe so. The problem is that this illusion is easier to pop than a juicy white pimple on your forehead—a couple of well placed words can do the trick.

So what's the solution? A defensive system that keeps us perpetually focused on the faults of others but lacks the ability to turn inward and recognize that we suffer from the same flaws. Somehow our situation involves endless excuses. Our self-justifying script is an endless litany of reasons that explain our behavior not as some internal bias but rather as a long list of external reasons. We believe we have intimate knowledge of the hows and whys of our actions and naturally conclude we are in full control.

Even when made wholly aware of how biased our thinking is, we're unable to avoid their power.

Researchers Emily Pronin and Matthew Kugler explained this as introspection illusion. Their research[27] showed that when subjects are asked to make judgments about themselves and others, they often displayed over inflated confidence about their abilities, appearance or personality traits (Dunning Kruger Bias). The experimenters then explained how the bias blind spot bias worked and how it may be affecting their judgments. Participants were then asked to re-evaluate themselves. Despite the expert explanation, subjects still rated themselves as less susceptible to bias than others. When asked why they were less susceptible, participants used a variety of reasons for why others were more biased than they were.

As much as we wish to know those around us; assumption, deduction and history can only take us so far. We will eventually reach a wall—whatever lies beyond is just speculation. There is a certain magic in this uncertainty of not knowing what others may do. As much as we might claim we are able to, we simply don't know the inner workings of others. We must rely on their overt behavior (outward) to see what they are really up to. We only see what is happening on the surface. We are oblivious to the sea of emotions, intentions, hopes and desires brewing underneath. It's pretty difficult to know what is going on under the water when we can only see the surface, especially, when it's not tropical water.

When we assess our own actions, the entire spectrum of emotions, thoughts and experiences is open to be reflected upon. However, our reflective search often comes up empty handed. Like a Trojan computer virus, biases operate unconsciously beyond the realm of cognition. They are the mental shortcuts that make the system work more efficiently, and this is why they are so damn sneaky.

Are you a good decision maker?

Perhaps you think that your superior intelligence will spare you from being humiliated when faced with your distorted self-perception, but unfortunately it doesn't. Boston University researcher Carey Morewedge found, "this susceptibility to the bias blind spot appears to be pervasive, and is unrelated to people's intelligence, self-esteem, and actual ability to make unbiased judgments and decisions."[20]

Again, we cannot see the disconnect between actual reality and our perception of it. Not only are we unaware of what is actually going on, we are less likely to WANT to learn from it. We ignore the advice of experts and those around us. We believe that their situations are somehow different from our own.

Perhaps this is why so many people are such bad listeners. The message behind the content is often lost and replaced by a keen focus on others' mistakes and shortcomings. How often is a friend's or loved one's message twisted into some elaborate evaluation of how biased or unfair their point of view is?

Availability Heuristic

Scenario 1: On her drive home, Judy likes to absentmindedly stare out her car window. She doesn't usually notice anything in particular. However on this day, she notices three or four houses in her neighborhood for sale. This surprises her and she brings it up later in a conversation with her husband. She says, "I can't believe how many houses are for sale around here. Maybe we should sell ours and move to a better neighborhood." The problem is there has been about the same amount of houses for sale in the neighborhood for at least five years.

Scenario 2: Steve heard that last week one of the employees in another department of his company was fired. He isn't sure why. A few days later, he saw a consultant whom he believes to be an efficiency expert. Steve is sure this means more layoffs and that he could possibly be the next in line.

"Memory is deceptive because it is colored by today's events." Albert Einstein

As I get older, my ability to forget things has continued to amaze me. Time spent with friends and relatives seems to blur. It all becomes labelled as things I might have done this year or the year before. Annual events come by and I am left shocked, thinking that I was in the same place at the same time last year doing the same thing. It somehow feels close and yet far away at the same time.

Our memory isn't optimized to remember things in the past with incredible detail and clarity. Rather, we only remember the gist of events and sometimes the salience of certain events or experiences is completely lost. We are biologically wired for the now. Our survival instincts have evolved to be hyperactive, pattern-detection machines that focus on the here and now. Our vast experience and history is not automatically factored into our decision-making process; rather, we weigh our judgments with the present information.

You may think being adaptable and flexible to the present moment is important; however, there needs to be a healthy balance between the past and the present for good decision making to take place. Good decision making means using past experience and knowledge as a reference point for future decision making rather than using whatever random information you have recently encountered.

Guess how many M&M'S are in the jar? 500? Wrong. 5000.

I remember once arguing with my mom that mowing the lawn would take me at least three hours. It seemed reasonable given the size of the front yard and how inept I was at using any kind of tool. The argument lasted for a while and eventually I set out to prove her wrong. My pride was thoroughly defeated when I realized it would only take about forty minutes including some wasted time looking for cool bugs under my mom's carefully planted garden stones.

We are not very good at guessing how long things will last or how frequently events occur together. This myopic tendency was beautifully researched in the late 1960s by Amos Tversky and Daniel Kahneman. Their availability heuristic bias soon found acceptance in most fields. Law, medicine, sociology, economics, and political science departments welcomed Kahneman and Tversky's idea that human logic suffered not from motivated irrationality but rather from this biologically wired cognitive bias. This was a big transition and science owes a huge thank you for this giant leap forward in acceptance and understanding.

It's pretty easy to see how we come up with some wild beliefs once we realize that people use this mental shortcut as the basis for decision making. The result is a little bit of compassion and understanding for people with entirely different belief systems once we realize they may not be wrong within their own perceptions of reality. Even when events don't occur at regular intervals, we are tricked into believing this illusory correlation.

In Kahneman's 1973 research[31], three motivating factors were proposed the availability heuristic: frequency of repetition, frequency of co-occurrence and illusory correlation. The first, how often something happens helps with retrieval. The more something happens, the more you remember it and the more important or "real" it may seem. Now, if you take any random phenomenon and repeat it within a certain context, associations are formed. These associations link the two instances together. In some cases, these links are very profound. Think of lucky charms (not the cereal) or weird rituals that baseball players might do before stepping up to bat. Maybe you feel like you need to snap your fingers twice before you come up to bat because you did it once and you were successful.

Kahneman's research showed that individuals used that strong association between two events to assess the frequency of future occurrences. This created a biased frequency judgement which was again reinforced by how many times the action was repeated in the future. Paired actions that are repeated encourage an even stronger association. So basically, you repeat the action over and over again until you really believe that the association is true, and that there can be no alternative. Eventually, this creates the illusory correlation we were talking about—the stronger the association between the two items, the more we think they are really correlated.

There is no better place to see this than in health fads. I'm sure everyone has a friend or co-worker who has advocated some crackpot crazy item for healthier living. Whether it's weight loss sunglasses, roundworms in your stomach, the sunlight diet, baby mice wine or just eating lots of margarine, it's pretty easy to see how someone could be influenced by the availability bias and actually think that engaging in a particular habit could be beneficial (these are actually all real diet methods).

I recently had an overweight co-worker tell me how much eating three tablespoons of raw organic honey was helping him avoid getting sick. Perhaps he didn't get sick for a while, but it definitely had nothing to do with his magic honey. The point is that it's pretty easy to come up with insane beliefs that you REALLY believe are true. Combine that with confirmation bias (only looking for evidence that supports your belief systems) and you have an excellent combination for self-deception.

"A clear conscience is usually the sign of bad memory."
Steven Wright

Advertisers always strive to inundate us with their jingles, slogans or product placement. Sometimes it seems that they are just wasting their time and money. You may think that you don't care about their product, and yet, advertisers keep spending millions to show you their merchandise? Actually have you noticed that even if you don't notice, you still notice?

Advertising firms employ psychologists and marketers who know that people judge the ease with which information is recalled as an ADDITIONAL source of information. Let me repeat this, it's important. Information that is recalled faster is deemed more relevant, more recent and much easier to remember. It's basically like your RAM memory on your computer. Our random access memories (RAM) are a mishmash of recent information, advertisements, gossip and other irrelevant information. Naturally, getting information from your RAM is a lot faster than using the hard drive.

Accessing those old memories where you might have made a really stupid decision and even regretted it for an entire day are a lot harder. Thinking about it often requires some sort of external reminder that encourages us to access our memory hard drive. This external reminder must make you thoughtfully examine the reliability of your current decision.

If we don't have this external reminder system in the form of a mother, wife, or TPS report (another Office Space reference), we are biased towards our RAM memory. This is the quick go-to memory and because it can be accessed faster, it actually becomes more important and influential. Our ease of access actual makes these memories even more believable.

Availability heuristics is all about how readily accessible and consumable information is, and nothing is more consumable than some tasty social media. The term "going viral" has become part of the everyday vernacular. Never before has a content producer been able to produce a piece of work that can generate millions of views in an impossibly short amount of time. It's the perfect medium to spread information that can truly change lives.

The problem is that it's also a wonderfully efficient medium to spreading nonsensical crap. If my overweight friend had a big enough audience and advocated eating three tablespoons of raw honey everyday (fifty-four grams of insulin spiking sugar), you might have a small army of disciples preaching the benefits of a chocolate bar a day fueled on nothing but raw bee vomit and the availability bias (honey is mostly bee vomit).

The Internet age is also the age of an overwhelming amount of low quality media and information that primes us into balkanizing into separate tribes where we believe our belief system somehow triumphs another. This is nothing new for humans, but it's been supercharged with the inter-connectivity of our modern world.

Emotionally charged content makes this effect even more powerful. Anything that is vivid, unusual or packed with emotionally latent material is given first class priority by our brains. These upgraded passengers are pretty big and may even require an extra few seats on the plane; much to the chagrin of our more rationally minded smaller passengers.

Decisions made in a more rational state of mind are quickly forgotten when an emotionally charged situation arises. Maybe you have been surfing and swimming at the beach for years without incident and have decided that based upon your years of experience, it's a pretty safe place. Then along comes a week of extremely graphic media coverage covering a spree of shark attacks. This shark-week report is pretty hard to get out of your head and before you know it, you're telling all your neighbors how dangerous the ocean is.

This is exactly what happened in the early 2000s. Media coverage on shark attacks excited a fearful public reaction, despite the fact that shark attacks actually deceased that year.[32] However, imagining the gaping, soulless eyes of a white shark as it cruelly chomps down on you while you were enjoying a naked midnight swim evokes a much more powerful emotional reaction than telling someone that they should be more worried about sinkholes than shark attacks (there were sixteen sinkhole deaths vs. eleven deaths from shark attacks between the years 1990 to 2006.[32])

The next time you start to think about sensational news coverage; instead, think about the availability bias. Instead of rationally weighing the evidence in its current and previous history, we are more apt to support the newer, flashier information. This in turn affects our perception of frequency. We see it once and think it happens all the time.

"Always do what you are afraid to do." Ralph Waldo Emerson

One of the most pervasive beliefs that is propagated by the media is in regards to violent events. Nothing captures the public's attention like a bit of blood and death. As terrible as violent crimes are, media coverage about them bias our perception towards their frequency.

One of my favorite TED talks involves linguist Steven Pinker and his presentation entitled, "The surprising decline of violence." He uses statistics to show that nearly every measure of violence and oppression is declining worldwide. The idea seems unconscionable but well researched statistics don't lie.

Availability bias serves to strengthen our belief systems that we in turn use to understand our reality and our world. It is hard to think about violence rationally when the mere mention of it lights up your reptilian brain. This brain region is called the amygdala and it is responsible for causing a person to experience fear and for helping the person to prepare to deal with potential emergency situations.

It's like an executive veto on any rational decision-making process. It's the thing that turns you into an Olympic sprinter when you're in danger before you even know what happened. When it comes to violence, the amygdala is the boss. It may be telling you the world is a violent place and you need to be careful. Yes, you certainly do. However, to what extent are you basing this perception of danger on media you have recently consumed?

I remember a time in early 2013 where I consumed a steady diet of nothing but conspiracy documentaries and reports. At the time, my friends' inability to see evidence of conspiracies all around them was beyond me. How can they think our water is safe! The Illuminati are everywhere! Don't they know there is a master race of lizard people calling all the shots!

The problem was my reality had become hyper focused on one belief system. My media consumption was the fuel for my distorted reality. Perhaps this is a slightly long-winded example, but you can see the role that availability bias could potentially play in the formation of personality cults where information is only disseminated from one source.

"The media's the most powerful entity on earth. They have the power to make the innocent guilty and to make

the guilty innocent, and that's power. Because they
control the minds of the masses." Malcolm X

The courtroom is predicated on the idea of fairness and equality. A strict protocol is followed to ensure that results are reviewed rationally and thoughtfully. The problem is that just being exposed to related events or information can "prime" jurors or judges into flawed thinking. Pre-trial exposure to media can make jurors more favorable or even harsher to plaintiffs. Researchers Landsman and Rakos[33] found that information presented in a slightly skewed summary would greatly impact the outcome of jurors' decisions.

In cases involving personal liability, individuals presented with negative information regarding a defendant found increased rates of liability. In a similar study, Garber (1998) found that an unusually high percentage of cases where plaintiffs were awarded punitive damages had greater media exposure than normal.[34]

Exposure to information before the trial has great potential to change how the civil or criminal litigation process works. This even happens when you think about how much money you'll be awarded for an accident. Do you know how much the going rate is for getting hit by a bus? I don't, but I can think of a few cases where people received a monstrous sum of money. These are the first examples that come to mind because they triggered an emotional reaction: surprise. The part that makes this tricky is that jurors don't generally know they are using previously available information to determine punishments or award compensation.

Availability bias can be a huge obstacle for most investors to get over. Unless you're a stock picker, which

I'm definitely not, watching too much financial media can be quite detrimental. I'm speaking for the average investor like myself, not a financial expert. When we watch too much financial media, the estimation problem comes up again. We use current information to predict the health of our financial decisions. It's pretty easy to panic when you think about the potential of losing all your money.

Availability bias isn't your friend when it comes to making long-term gains. We are biologically programmed for loss aversion (not losing what we have) and greedy for big gains. In a 2012 report by Franklin Templeton[32] entitled *Global Investor Sentiment Survey 1,* participants were asked how they believed the S&P 500 Index performed in 2009, 2010 and 2011. Results showed that 66 percent of respondents viewed the market as flat or dead in 2009, 48 percent said the same for 2010 and 53 percent believed this in 2011.

The reality was actually quite different. The S&P 500 earned 26.5 percent in 2009, 15.1 percent in 2010 and 2.1 percent in 2011. The information that was previously available (during the 2007–2008 market crash) and all the surrounding media hype were enough to misinform investors who could have easily checked the actual returns in a couple of clicks.

Status Quo Bias and the Fear of Choice

Scenario 1: Judy has been using the same insurance company for the last twenty years. She recently heard her coworkers talking about another company that offered much lower rates than what she was paying. She had even seen ads on the Internet advertising a 30 percent lower price than the company she is currently using. She thinks about changing companies, but is immediately deterred by the thought of dealing with the required paperwork. Instead, she elects to continue using the same company.

Scenario 2: Steve's wife has sent him to the store to buy a couple of groceries. One of the items is soap. After an exhaustive search through all seventeen aisles, he finally finds the soap section. He is surprised to find more than one hundred brands of soap and they all vary in price. There is organic, natural, naturally organic, Brazilian, French, non-scented and organically scented as well as many more. He is confused by all the choices. He just wants soap. He spends a few minutes picking up random bars of soap and eventually takes the one that the customer beside him also took.

> *"When people have too many choices, they make bad choices." Thom Browne*

Have you ever been to a restaurant where there are so many choices on the menu that you just feel confused? Maybe you decide to get the beef brisket but then see a beef brisket sandwich and a beef brisket salad. Suddenly, you're not sure which one you should order. If you are hungry, this confusion is compounded and you end up just ordering a hamburger like every other time. Contrast this to a restaurant that offers only chicken, beef or fish. The choices are simple. There is no second guessing yourself or worrying that you might have missed out on something more delicious.

The idea that more freedom in the form of choices makes us happier is a big fallacy. In most cases, having fewer options increases our freedom. This can be seen across a huge spectrum of applications ranging from sales to design. Good design tells us what we should do. We like being told what to do. We like not thinking; that's why we usually object from any deviation from the current situation. Our preference for our current state of affairs over any potential change is the last cognitive bias we will discuss— the status quo bias.

Often, we encounter a situation that is more beneficial than our current one; however, we are slow to adopt it. Are we just lazy? Stubborn? Or perhaps we crave the security and comfort that the present situation provides? There may be something better out there but the outcome is not entirely certain.

A recent study by psychologists Mark Lepper and Sheena Iyengar[35] tested this paradox of choice. Researchers set up two stands in a gourmet food store displaying various jams. The first stand had twenty-four varieties while the second one had only six. Samplers tried the same amount of jams, but when it came to actually buying the jams, there was a massive difference. Thirty percent of people exposed to the smaller six-jar stand made a purchase whereas only 3 percent bought something from the stand with more variety. This is great food for thought. Maybe having it "your way" isn't the best sales strategy.

This is our primitive side. The entrenched need for us to follow the majority opinion is built into the system. We are social animals by nature and to mimic what others are doing feels right. Deviating away from the status quo is a heavy cognitive load and not something lightly undertaken by most people. It's just so much easier to follow what other people are doing. Sometimes, just following what others are doing is a wonderful feeling. Not having to worry about all the little things that might come up or just being willfully ignorant to them lets us spend more time doing the things that matter—like using Facebook.

"The status quo sucks." George Carlin

Maintaining the status quo is actually the safest option as long as the previous decisions were "good enough." There is no need to rock the boat with crazy ideas or decisions. The problem is that if we don't rock the boat, too many things get stagnant and your mind becomes less open to new possibilities.

The outcome of a change is not certain, and deviating from the status quo could result in absolute disaster or total success. Some errors are just more costly than others. Imagine if you worked in an office for the past ten years and decided to quit and start your own business. This is a big decision and most people would be hesitant to jump into a life-changing venture; especially, if they are older or have dependents. You might maintain the same standard of life, go totally bankrupt or make more than you have ever dreamed of. Maybe this is what makes you so hesitant to try new things? It's a gamble, and our brains are wired for safety, NOT for adventure.

Have you ever tried something in the spirit of adventurousness and been thoroughly disappointed? Maybe you usually order chicken fried rice, but today you decide to try chicken feet. You may enjoy eating a chicken's deep fried feet but chances are most of us will regret our adventurous decision; especially, if we are hungry.

When faced with two options, one that is tested and safe and another that is unknown, sometimes picking the unknown option causes more regret. It's easy to feel upset about a decision when you know that the alternative was safe and good. You may think to yourself, "Why did I do that!" or "Next time, I will definitely not do that."

These feelings are powerful motivators to do the same thing as you have always done. Kahneman[33] found that, "more regret is experienced when a decision changes the status quo than when it maintains it. Together, these forces provide an advantage for the status quo; people are motivated to do nothing or to maintain current or previous decisions."

Have you ever experienced something which you initially viewed as absolutely terrible, but later realized it was a great change? A lot of people feel this way about being laid-off after deciding to pursue their dream job. While many of us may not be so lucky, I think we can all agree that breaking the status quo can result in unexpected results.

If you are like me, being indecisive comes naturally. Should I do this or that? I really don't know, I may as well wait a while and decide later. That waiting results in me not deciding and feeling anxious. Our brains are programmed for simplicity. We want to avoid making difficult decisions.

Researchers at the University College London have conducted an experiment which looks at the neural pathways involved in decision making.[34] Their results showed that the more difficult a situation is, the more likely we are not to act. The study examined the decision-making ability of participants playing a fictional tennis "line judgment" game. As they played, their brains were scanned using an fMRI (functional magnetic resonance imager).

Subjects were asked to engage in two tasks. The first task involved looking at a cross located between two lines on a screen while simultaneously holding down the default key. While continuing to hold down the key, they had to decide if the ball was in or out. The computer would then tell them whether the ball was IN or OUT. The second task required them to decide if the computer's in/out call was correct. To accept it as being correct, they had to hold down the default key to accept the call or release it and change to another key to reject it. Results showed a strong bias towards just holding the default key down regardless of the ball's position.

Even when the computer was clearly wrong, people were still hesitant to acknowledge it. As the times were increased, this effect became even more obvious. The results from the fMRI showed that difficult decision making involved higher activation of the subthalamic nucleus which is believed to play a key role in overcoming the status quo bias.

Should you stay or go.

So the next time you feel indecisive or want to avoid making a big change in your life, remember that this bias is programmed into you. Deviating from a situation that already provides safety isn't an evolutionary smart thing to do. The primitive mind thinks why travel somewhere else if we have an abundance of fish and berries here? Our brains

72

aren't wired for being adventurous and trying new things. We are wired for safety and the routines that ensure it.

Guess the Bias

In this next section, I will use various examples and conversations. Your job is to determine which cognitive bias is affecting judgment. There may be more than one cognitive bias. After you spot the bias, try to take some time to reflect on it and see if you have experienced it.

Situation 1: Bob works at a local company and is a strong supporter of the idea that the human race is controlled by a master race of lizards. He is certain of the legitimacy of his claims and often argues with his coworkers regarding the undeniably obvious evidence. The problem is he only watches Lizard TV, a pro-lizard, overlord-sponsored network where viewers receive news reports and information that is entirely biased towards the lizard conspiracy. Bob sometimes watches other news networks but immediately dismisses most of them as propagating false information.

Situation 2: Steve is looking for a new car. He is looking for a simple family van and hopes to buy one second hand. He has a particular model in mind, and according to his research, the going price for the van is $3000. Upon meeting the car salesman, Steve is introduced to the limited edition version of the car he wants to buy. There is a substantial price markup on the van. It is priced at $9000. The price, three times more than he expected, shocks him. However, he quickly overcomes his shock when he learns that the basic models are only slightly higher than his original price range. The vans at the dealership are priced at $4000. Steve agrees to buy a second-hand model for $4000.

Situation 3: Cindy is sick of arguing with her boyfriend. They are both stubborn people and have an itchy trigger finger for anything they deem to be unfair. They often get into huge arguments that build into shouting matches that can last for hours. They are both exceptionally talented at recalling previous incidents where one of them was overly unfair or biased. Cindy thinks her boyfriend, John, lacks the ability to see how ignorant he is about certain points which are crystal clear to her. She feels that if John had the same level of clarity and honesty as she has, they wouldn't argue as much.

Situation 4: John works in the sales department. He likes his job but he likes his lunch break even more. He usually spends his lunch break chatting with his coworkers. Last week, John noticed how awkward one of his coworkers was toward him. She didn't look at him when she spoke and she only responded to questions with a few words. John later spoke about this to several people. John told them that he thought she was impolite, unprofessional and not very friendly. His later interactions with her were slightly tainted by this impression.

Situation 5: Steve has been complaining about his boss, Mr. Smith, for a few years. Mr. Smith is the head of the marketing department and has been working at the company since he was twenty. Now, he's sixty-five. Steve thinks that Mr. Smith's marketing methods and management are totally outdated. He doesn't pay attention to social media and still insists on using billboard advertisements on the side of the highway despite the fact that most people are busy looking at their cell phones. At one point, Steve and several coworkers present marketing research that indicates they could make dramatic improvements if they made a few changes. Mr. Smith responded, "This is the way I've been doing things for forty-five years. This is the way things work." Why is Mr. Smith still running the show?

Situation 6: John and Steve are brothers. They are both overweight, but John works out regularly and has maintained a consistent weight throughout his adult life. Steve hasn't done so well. He is constantly reminded by his doctor that at his age, his physical health should be of utmost importance. Steve understands this very well. He follows a diet, has a personal trainer and eats all manner of health food. The problem is that he just can't stick to it longer than a month. He will often tell himself that he will accept a short break from his health regime in order to indulge in something now. These little indulgences have compounded over time.

Situation 7: Cindy has told her daughter that she can't go out with her friends. Cindy's daughter is thoroughly confused because two weeks ago she was allowed to go out. Cindy explains that she just doesn't feel comfortable with her daughter being out so late. When asked the reason, Cindy makes mention of a recent mugging that happened in their city. Cindy watches the news every night and this topic has been thoroughly reported on. The problem is that muggings usually occur in their city and this has never stopped Cindy from letting her daughter go out with friends.

Situation 8: Billy and his girlfriend love to watch live debates. Recently, they have been watching debates about economics. Billy is quick to give his opinion on a recent bill that requires health care providers to pay more money. He is confident in his opinion despite not having any evidence or research to back it up. He continuously argues his point even though he is wrong most of the time. If asked to take a survey, he would score incredibly high in perceived knowledge and utterly lacking in actual knowledge.

Situation 9: Steve and his wife are approaching retirement. They have both worked for the government nearly all their lives. They are getting ready to cash in their pension but there's a problem. The retirement fund they are currently using was decided on in 1965 when they first started working. The economy was a lot different in 1965 and the majority of their savings are in the form of government bonds. However, the market has changed a lot since 1965 and for the last twenty years, bonds have been performing terribly. Steve and his wife are still reluctant to change their plans despite the evidence.

Situation 10: Steve has always wanted to open his own ice cream shop. His genius idea was to sell ice cream that was flavored like vegetables. He included everyone's favorite vegetable like bitter gourd, spinach, horseradish and, of course, onion. Steve also uses high-fat natural cream. He thought that since the Paleo Diet craze has become more and more popular, his high-fat, vegetable ice cream would be an instant success. Sixty thousand dollars and three bank loans later as well as after working ten hours a week for two years, Steve is feeling very frustrated. Much to the disappointment of his wife, he insists that he can't give up the business. He has already invested so much into it. He is sure the business will be successful despite utterly failing for the past two years.

Answers and Remedies

1. Confirmation Bias

Bob clearly watches too much Lizard TV. His lizard overlords have primed him with too much information that supports this view. Maybe if he watched some other news networks, he could develop a more well-rounded opinion.

2. Anchoring

Although Bob had an original price in mind, it was quickly replaced. The first piece of information you are exposed to often becomes your starting point to assess subsequent information. In this case, the salesperson did an excellent job of setting a price that was just way too high. As a result, the $4000 Bob agreed on seemed totally reasonable.

3. Bias Blind Spot

Cindy's boyfriend might be unfair and biased but there is a high chance that Cindy is equally biased. Her boyfriend's mistakes seem like great evidence of his flawed cognition, but until she further examines herself, she won't know if she suffers from the same mistakes. Seeing other people's ignorance is always a lot easier than turning the magnifying glass inwards.

4. Fundamental Attribute Error (FAE)

Judging a book by its cover or, in this case, a human by his face is always tricky business. We are privy to our inner feelings and motivations (sometimes) but formulating the reasons behind other people's behaviour is pure speculation. Like investing in a random stock based on how it's performing recently, we are taking good decision making and replacing it with guesswork. As we mentioned, the engine behind FAE is the need to simplify the world through mental shortcuts. The problem with taking shortcuts is that sometimes we end up in the wrong place.

5. Survivorship Bias

There is an innate tendency to associate age with quality and taste. What makes an old muscle car more appealing? Is it the fact that many of them are poorly constructed compared to today's automobiles, are less safe and guzzle gas as fast as a Humvee? Or is it simply because they are rarer and somehow cooler? Either way, the past doesn't always represent the pinnacle of wisdom or progress. The things in the past aren't as awesome as they were *back in the day*. The same goes for Mr. Smith's antiqued marketing techniques. While he is wasting money on trucks driving around town blaring advertisements, his competitors are using smart social marketing.

6. Hyperbolic Discounting

They say patience is a virtue. John and Steve would certainly agree; however, their actions might not follow suit. In this case, Steve just can't resist the temptations of an occasional chicken wing even when it turns into twenty. You might recognize examples of this from your own life. How many of us don't bother saving money when we know we should. It's hard to budget a portion for later when the entire world is screaming YOLO (you only live once).

7. Availability Bias

You are what you eat. And if you eat crappy media, well, guess what happens. Cindy has clearly watched too much news. Bite-sized bits of data have hijacked her brain into doing something that her rational self and her daughter would otherwise disapprove of. She knows that she lives in a safe environment but she just can't shake the feeling that her daughter going out might be dangerous.

8. Dunning Kruger Bias

Unless you took a test about everything you know, you probably wouldn't realize how much you don't know. Since we aren't students in China, we aren't exposed to rigorous testing. Instead, we are left to our own intuitions about our expertise—just like Billy. The thing about intuitions is that they are self-supporting. We have been taught from childhood that we are great, and this inflated self-confidence serves as the launch platform for real competency.

9. Status Quo Bias and a Sprinkle of Survivorship Bias

We are naturally inclined to avoid the pain of decision making. Sometimes making a decision isn't even painful, but the apprehension that leads up to it may be too much for some people to handle. Our acceptance of change gets stifled as we age and our habits become more ingrained. This status-quo effect extends itself into every facet of life. Being adventurous is not programmed into our brains, but survival is. Sticking to a safe predictable habit is a great way to ensure safety. However, it isn't great for ensuring progress or adaptive change. Perhaps Steve should have been a bit more flexible with his investment decisions instead of staying with what was the standard advice in the 1960s.

Our sprinkle of survivorship bias comes in the form of that investment style. When Steve received his investment advice, there were a multitude of people who benefitted tremendously from a mostly bond-based investment. What worked in the past isn't necessarily helpful in the future. In this case, it's the opposite of what he should be doing.

10. Sunk Cost Fallacy

You need to know when to call it quits. You might be thinking of all those inspiring quotes you learned in school about never quitting, but there are exceptions to this rule. Exceptions are exceptionally important when a failing endeavour is slowly sucking your financial resources dry or draining your relationships. Someone needs to slap Steve and tell him no one will eat onion flavored ice cream, regardless of how much bacon grease and raw vegetables Paleo-diet enthusiasts want to eat.

I Must Congratulate You.

I hope that everyone was able to successfully identify the above ten examples. I realize this book isn't a voluminous four-hundred-page tome about every manner of cognitive bias in the world. However, if you have read up to this point, you are basically an expert compared to the majority of the population.

Not only were you able to get through my unprofessional writing style, you are clearly interested in learning how to think more rationally. You are awesome, not because you bought this book (which I hope you did), but because you showed a unique, rarely displayed interest in learning the errors of your own cognition—biologically based biases that come with all the bells and whistles of your human brain.

You may think many people are interested in becoming smarter and more cognitively competent; however, I would disagree. Challenging yourself is difficult and it all starts with the will to improve yourself. For this, I must wholeheartedly congratulate you.

Congratulations! You are a winner!

I Must Apologize To You.

Perhaps you thought that I would provide you with actionable steps to get rid of your cognitive biases. If I had the ability to change your physical genetic makeup and rearrange your brain circuitry, I would almost certainly charge more than $3.99. Unfortunately, my words or examples cannot change you. You are biased and will probably remain biased for the majority of your life. The answer is simple. It's your brain's fault. In an attempt to build your confidence and simplify your world, we have been bestowed the gift of cognitive biases—one of our many survival mechanisms.

So I must apologize if any of my readers believed I would provide a surefire way to change their anatomy. I can't, nor would I want to. Biases are not all bad and evil. They serve to simplify and sometimes those simplifications lead to complications and biased thinking; however, most of the time our mental heuristics (shortcuts) provide us with a smooth, steady ride through life. Our biases are like our consistency editors ironing out the bumps and rough edges in our movie called life.

Don't Forget The Story

"The more you know yourself, the more patience you have for what you see in others." Erik Erikson

Well, that about concludes our little course. I know I only covered ten biases and there are many more. If you want a more complete listing, I suggest you take a look at the Wikipedia cognitive bias list. There are over forty biases listed there.

I do hope that I have instilled an appreciation for how entrenched our biases are. They are built into our operating system and are difficult, if not impossible, to change. You can't overcome or change your biology.

I should clarify that biases aren't necessarily bad. They may encourage flawed thinking, but most of the time, they serve as mental shortcuts that allow us to navigate the world easier. So, if you are wondering how to get rid of your biases, I think you may have slightly missed the point.

Let's review what we have learned so far. What do biases actually do?

1. They serve to limit information and simplify an otherwise overly complex world.

2. They help expedite reasoning and decision making.

3. They also serve to keep us safe by making heuristic rules of thumb that can be applied to most situations.

4. They serve to create a partially fictitious sense of confidence and autonomy upon which competence can be built more effectively.

Like Brain Corp. where all the employees report directly to Mr. Brain, our own minds work similarly. Information is limited to fit within the confines of the company culture. Superfluous information is casually disregarded to streamline the process.

You may need to make an immediate decision about whether something is safe, cheap or effective and as a result, you need to rely on initial information or more readily accessible information. But ignoring the entirety of the available information or over-focusing on more accessible information is responsible for biased perception.

Safe and Sound.

Making the world orderly and easily understandable is something everyone needs. Have you ever experienced something that you just can't understand? Why would someone do that? The words, "it just doesn't make sense" echo over and over in your mind.

Uncertainty is like an annoying mosquito buzzing by your ear while you attempt to sleep. We all crave resolution. Whether we actually get that resolution or create a narrative that explains it, it serves the same purpose—to simplify things.

We talked about our need to create linear relationships (A causes B). Our innate need for a "just world" reflects a deep need for the world to be orderly and understandable. Biases serve to create this order and give us a neatly explained world which is smooth around the edges. Order creates the perception of safety.

We also seek clarity through our personal narrative. The story of who we are and what kind of world we live in provides a roadmap to the whys and hows. Our narrative acts as a personal mirror to the world. We see through it and see the world reflected back at us. The world is made to fit into our story.

Don't Forget, You Are Awesome.

When we discussed the Dunning Kruger bias, I showed you the gap between actual ability and perceived ability. I'm sure this is something easily recognizable within our own lives. We all know a totally incompetent co-worker who has a hyper-inflated sense of confidence or worth.

If you look deep enough, you might find a bit of the old Dunning Kruger bias in you too. You might find this bias because it's a remnant of childhood and is a required method to build actual competence and confidence. Think of these two situations. Both involve people who are incompetent at what they are doing, but they don't realize how unskilled they actually are.

Situation 1: Little Billy comes up to you and tells you that he can show you how to do absolutely anything on the Internet. He says, "Ya, it's so easy for me. Let me show you" as his seven-year-old legs dangle off the computer chair. You think to yourself, "Awww, he is so cute."

Situation 2: Larry has invited himself into your office and explained that the way you are using WordPress (a website program) is totally wrong. He says, "I'm an expert at this program, I can do anything with it." As he sits down on your computer chair, you think to yourself, "Hey, Larry, %$#% off. I don't need your help."

Overconfidence is cute in a child but when adults display the same over-inflated confidence, it comes off as pretentious and foolish. Think of the financial advisors we talked about who lacked actual financial competence despite believing themselves to be highly qualified.

What I Got From Learning I Am Stupid

It wasn't so much through researching or reading about cognitive bias that I began to notice how judgmental I was, but rather through mindfulness. Mindfulness is defined as a mental state achieved by focusing one's awareness on the present moment while acknowledging and accepting one's feelings, thoughts and bodily sensations.

My own process of mindfulness didn't involve a guru or any sort of sudden realization, but rather with self-learning. It started with research and authors who explained the complicated nature of our human biology and how it has wonderfully deceived us into being sociable yet ignorant.

At first, it amazed me how biases were intertwined with every facet of my life. The more I learned about them, the more I could see them everywhere. They were like little gremlins creeping and popping their cute ugly heads around every conversation and opinion. My knowledge made me even more sensitive to others' biases. I felt I could see the errors in others' judgment even more clearly with my new knowledge.

Basically I became an overly confident, overly analytic observer of others. This is a dangerous path to walk on. People don't like to be challenged or to be shown their cognitive errors. It wasn't until I found a group of skeptics online, specifically a podcast called Skeptics Guide to the Universe, that I began to question my own belief systems instead of those around me.

These questions led to a deep introspective dive where I basically spent three to four months with a book glued to my hand. I was surprised by how many of the great writers and philosophers of ancient history echoed the same scientific findings that show how incredibly biased we all are. Our modern world has provided us with a way to qualify these results and pass them onto future generations, but the same principles and lessons can still be taught by reading great works of literature or philosophy. The only difference is the accessibility. Reading a four-hundred-page book or trying to decipher philosophy hasn't exactly been popular goals. Science has granted ordinary people like me the ability to see these biases in action in simpler and quantified terms.

I hope you have gained some insight into your own mind by reading this book. In writing it, I realize that the biggest lesson I learned was how to be compassionate. We may differ on the surface but our biology dictates that we are all fundamentally wired the same. Seeing how unreasonable, stubborn and otherwise blind I can be about some things allowed me to see the same errors in others.

Remember, I have only talked about ten of the many biases that we all have. I think that since you are reading this book, you are one of the few people who will succeed in learning to think more rationally and, as a result, more compassionately.

So let me give everyone one last mission before we end. Now that you are equipped with a slightly better understanding of your own mind, try to find biases within your own life. Our first reaction may be to go find them in others, and although this may be easy to do, don't.

Instead, focus on yourself. The reason is simple. It's much easier to see how biased you are than to accurately judge others. Once you understand the errors in your own decision-making process, seeing them in others will not be tainted by judgement.

The final part is telling them they are wrong…if you want. But I will leave that to your good judgment. Good luck.

A Couple of Other Great Books

I hope everyone enjoyed this book and if you want to know more, I can definitely suggest some great titles. I have been reading about this stupidity/self knowledge genre for a few years now. Some great books you might want to pick up include the following:

Predictably Irrational by Dan Ariely

The Upside of Irrationality by Dan Ariely

You Are Now So Smart by David McRaney

You Are Now Less Dumb by David McRaney

The Invisible Gorilla by Christopher Chabris

Endnotes

1. Northcraft, Gregory B; Neale, Margaret A (1987). "Experts, amateurs, and real estate: An anchoring-and-adjustment perspective on property pricing decisions". *Organizational Behavior and Human Decision Processes* **39** (1): 84–97.
2. Schkade, D. A.; Kahneman, D. (1998). "Does Living in California Make People Happy? A Focusing Illusion in Judgments of Life Satisfaction". *Psychological Science* **9** (5): 340–346.
3. Janiszewski, Chris; Uy, Dan (2008). "Precision of the Anchor Influences the Amount of Adjustment". *Psychological Science* **19** (2): 121–127
4. Oechssler, Jörg; Roider, Andreas; Schmitz, Patrick W. (2009). "Cognitive abilities and behavioral biases". *Journal of Economic Behavior & Organization* **72** (1): 147–152
5. Nickerson, Raymond S. (1998), "Confirmation Bias; A Ubiquitous Phenomenon in Many Guises", *Review of General Psychology* (Educational Publishing Foundation)**2** (2): 175–220
6. Baron, Jonathan (2000), *Thinking and deciding* (3rd ed.), New York: Cambridge University Press, ISBN 0-521-65030-5
7. Snyder, Mark; Swann, Jr., William B. (1978), "Hypothesis-Testing Processes in Social Interaction", *Journal of Personality and Social Psychology* (American Psychological Association) **36** (11): 1202–1212, doi:10.1037/0022-3514.36.11.1202
8. Oswald, Margit E.; Grosjean, Stefan (2004), "Confirmation Bias", in Pohl, Rüdiger F., *Cognitive*

Illusions: A Handbook on Fallacies and Biases in Thinking, Judgement and Memory, Hove, UK: Psychology Press, pp. 79–96

9. Westen, Drew; Blagov, Pavel S.; Harenski, Keith; Kilts, Clint; Hamann, Stephan (2006), "Neural Bases of Motivated Reasoning: An fMRI Study of Emotional Constraints on Partisan Political Judgment in the 2004 U.S. Presidential Election

10. Ross, Lee; Anderson, Craig A. (1982), "Shortcomings in the attribution process: On the origins and maintenance of erroneous social assessments", in Kahneman, Daniel; Slovic, Paul; Tversky, Amos, *Judgment under uncertainty: Heuristics and biases*, Cambridge University Press, pp. 129–152

11. Plous, Scott (1993), *The Psychology of Judgment and Decision Making*, McGraw-Hill

12. Haith AM; Reppert TR; Shadmehr. (2012), "Evidence for hyperbolic temporal discounting of reward in control of movements", Journal of Neuroscience

13. Mischel, Walter; Ebbesen, Ebbe B.; Raskoff Zeiss, Antonette (1972). "Cognitive and attentional mechanisms in delay of gratification.". *Journal of Personality and Social Psychology* **21** (2): 204–218

14. Schultz, W; Dayan, P; Montague, PR. A neural substrate of prediction and reward, Science (1997) March 14th.

15. Why Losers Have Delusions of Grandeur". *New York Post*. 23 May 2010. Retrieved 19 March 2014

16. Dunning, David. We Are All Confident Idiots. Pacific Standard. Oct 27 2014

17. Morris, Errol (20 June 2010). "The Anosognosic's Dilemma: Something's Wrong but You'll Never Know

What It Is (Part 1)". *New York Times*. Retrieved 7 March 201

18. Kruger, Justin; Dunning, David (1999). "Unskilled and Unaware of It: How Difficulties in Recognizing One's Own Incompetence Lead to Inflated Self-Assessments". *Journal of Personality and Social Psychology* **77** (6): 1121–34

19. http://www.usfinancialcapability.org/

20. Hodges, B. Regehr, G. Martin, D. "Difficulties in recognizing one's own incompetence: novice physicians who are unskilled and unaware of it.". U.S. National Library of Medicine, Oct 7 2001

21. Kahneman, D. (2011). Thinking, fast and slow. Farrar, Straus and Giroux.

22. Ariely, D. (2009). Predictably irrational, revised and expanded edition: The hidden forces that shape our decisions. Harper

23. Max H. Bazerman: *Negotiating Rationally* January 1, 1994

24. Höffler, Felix. "Why Humans Care About Sunk Costs While (Lower) Animals Don't." The Max Planck Institute for Research on Collective Goods, 31 Mar. 2008. Web. Mar. 2011.

25. McRaney, David. The Sunk Cost Fallacy. March 25 2011. www.youarenotsosmart.com

26. Lerner, M. J., & Miller, D. T. (1977). Just-world research and the attribution process: Looking back and ahead.*Psychological Bulletin*, *85*, 1030-1051.

27. Reeder, G.D., (1982). Let's give the fundamental attribution error another chance. Journal of Personality and Social Psychology, 43(2), 341-34

28. Masuda, T.; Ellsworth, P. C.; Mesquita, B.; Leu, J.; Tanida, S.; van de Veerdonk, E. (2008). "Placing the

face in context: Cultural differences in the perception of facial emotion"

29. Mangel, Marc; Samaniego, Francisco (June 1984). "Abraham Wald's work on aircraft survivability". *Journal of the American Statistical Association* **79** (386): 259–267

30. Elton; Gruber; Blake (1996). "Survivorship Bias and Mutual Fund Performance". *Review of Financial Studies* **9** (4): 1097–1120

31. Tversky, Amos; Kahneman, Daniel (1973). "Availability: A heuristic for judging frequency and probability".*Cognitive Psychology* **5** (2): 207–232

32. Franklin Templeton Investments. "Investors Should Beware The Role of 'Availability Bias'". Business Insider. Oct. 6, 2012. Dec. 1, 2013

33. Fleming, Stephen; C. Thomas; R. Dolan (February 2010). "Overcoming Status Quo Bias in the Human Brain".*Proceedings of the National Academy of Sciences of the United States of America* **107** (13): 6005–6009

34. Fleming, Stephen; C. Thomas; R. Dolan (February 2010). "Overcoming Status Quo Bias in the Human Brain".*Proceedings of the National Academy of Sciences of the United States of America* **107** (13): 6005–6009

Printed in Great Britain
by Amazon